WEIRD
CANADIAN WORDS
How to Speak Canadian

Edrick Thay

FOLK LORE PUBLISHING

The Publisher: Folklore Publishing
Website: www.folklorepublishing.com

Library and Archives Canada Cataloguing in Publication

Thay, Edrick, 1977–
   Weird Canadian words / by Edrick Thay.

(Great Canadian stories)
Includes bibliographical references.
ISBN 13: 978-1-894864-32-9
ISBN 10: 1-894864-32-8

   1. Canadianisms (English) 2. English language—
   Etymology. I. Title. II. Series.

PE3231.T48 2004 422   C2004-907020-7

Project Director: Faye Boer
Production: Trina Koscielnuk

We acknowledge the financial support of the Alberta Foundation for the Arts and the Government of Canada through the Book Publishing Industry Development Program for our publishing activities.

Canadian   Patrimoine
Heritage   canadien

PC: P5

Table of Contents

Dedication

To the boys of the Boxing Day Classic

Acknowledgements

As always, I would like to thank the people at Folklore Publishing for their help on this book, notably. For her sure editing hand, Sandra Bit deserves my gratitude and thanks to Trina Koscielnuk for her work on the layout.

I would also like to extend my thanks to my brother, Eldwin Thay, on whose futon I crashed while researching and writing this book. For bolstering my spirits during the most taxing and stressful of moments, I extend my thanks again to my fellow writer-in-arms, Dan Asfar. I would also like to acknowledge Nick Protti, Bonnie Kar, Michelle Chew and Tessa Kroeker for their ideas and insights.

Introduction

GROWING UP, I'D NEVER really given much thought to words that were distinctly Canadian. I knew that as a Canadian, I was supposed to say "eh" a lot, but that was about it. It wasn't until I lived in the United States that it became quite clear that Canadian English has a vocabulary all its own. Beyond the squeals of delight every time I said "eh" and peals of laughter that erupted every time my friends asked me to say, "out and about in the house," I found that Americans were unfamiliar with many words that I took for granted. Words like tuque, two-four, gaunch and Bloody Caesar only drew confused stares. The words I spoke marked me as foreign, different, and most importantly, like my passport, the words marked me as a Canadian.

When I began research for this book, I started with those words most commonly associated by foreigners with Canadians—words like hoser, Canuck, and of course, the ubiquitous eh. But as I dug deeper, I began uncovering terms whose origins surprised me. I'd little idea that the Bloody Caesar had been invented in my home province of Alberta (I'd always believed that it had been conceived in the Las Vegas casino of the same name) and was stunned to learn that hat trick was a term derived not from hockey, but from that most British of sports, cricket. What became clear to me as I wrote is that Canadian English, like any other language, is a symbol of our history, our past and our identity. And while many believe that little differentiates Canadian culture from American culture (a reasonable assumption since we watch their movies and their television programs, eat at their restaurants, consume their goods and listen to their music), the language of Canadians reveals just how unique a nation we inhabit.

Although hat trick may not be uniquely Canadian, many others associated with our national pastime are. Terms like five-hole, puck and even hockey may have murky roots, but they are most certainly Canadian in origin—a reflection of our great national obsession. Our language reveals us to be a great nation of innovators. Canadians invented the snowmobile, the paint roller, the Macintosh apple, Trivial Pursuit and Medicare. Inventions such as Marquis Wheat and the Yukon Gold potato had an indelible impact upon the development, expansion and evolution of our country. Without Marquis Wheat, the western prairies may have remained forever inhospitable to settlers, and Canada would be without its breadbasket.

Canada is a diverse nation that borders three oceans—the Pacific, Atlantic and Arctic. As a result, idioms and terms are specific to each region, from British Columbia (where Chinook jargon has given rise to many terms in common use today) to Ontario (where many of its idioms reflect its strong British heritage) and from Québec (where its love for food and Gallic heritage are mirrored in terms like creton, poutine and cipaille) to the Maritimes (where a host of words, like ballicater and gaspereau, reveal those provinces' close ties to their nautical traditions) and finally, to the north (from where aboriginal words like inuksuk and kayak have entered Canadian English).

Many of these words may be familiar, but I hope that the origins and usage of some few might lead to smiles of surprise and delight, and that this volume gives more than a fleeting glimpse at the sociology of our history and that it deepens an understanding of our culture.

ACADIA and ACADIAN

Historically, an Acadian was a native of the original French colony of Acadia. Today, an Acadian is any French-speaking descendent of the early French settlers of that colony. Those settlers are probably best remembered for being the victims of a nasty and spiteful mass expulsion at the hands of the British in the mid-1700s. Acadia was established by France in 1604, initially at Port Royal, presently Annapolis Royal, Nova Scotia. That colony later grew to encompass all the land between the Atlantic Ocean and the St. Lawrence River, including what is today southeastern Québec, eastern Maine, Nova Scotia, New Brunswick and Prince Edward Island. From the early 1600s to the early 1700s, Acadians lived contentedly under French rule, although the British made noises for years about wanting them gone. Unfortunately, after losing the French and Indian War (1754–63), France surrendered Acadia to Britain in 1763 as part of the Treaty of Paris. But the deportation and exile of many thousands of French Acadians to other parts of North America, France and England had already begun in 1755. When the war ended in 1763, the exile was technically over, after which some Acadians tried to return to their homes. They soon discovered that their land had been settled by others, so there was no going back. Exiled Acadians resettled in various places in the eastern U.S. and Canada and abroad, but perhaps the best known group settled in Louisiana, and their descendants became known as Cajun. In 2004, Acadians around the world celebrated Acadie 2004, the 400th anniversary of the arrival and settlement of the French in Acadia.

ACCLAMATION

From the Latin word *acclamare*, to shout, acclamation has been in use since the mid-16th century. It usually means a shout of enthusiastic approval or a vote taken without a formal ballot. In Canada, acclamation is a political term referring to an unopposed election win; a political victory by default owing to a lack of opposition.

ALBERTA CLIPPER

The Alberta Clipper is reviled through much of the American plains for its high winds, snow and frigid temperatures. It was named for the clipper ship, a very fast sailing vessel—the word clipper itself was derived from the verb *to clip*, or to move quickly. The Alberta Clipper can attain speeds of 60 km/h, with gusts approaching 100 km/h. Born from a low pressure zone that forms over Alberta, the Alberta Clipper dives southeast into the Dakotas and Minnesota and then eastward to the Great Lakes, dropping light, powdery snow and temperatures along the way. Should it cross the Appalachians, as it sometimes does, the Alberta Clipper becomes a nor'easter, with winds notorious for their snows and high winds. The Alberta Clipper's effects have been felt as far south as Texas.

ALBERTITE

In the mid-19th century, a black substance with a bright and glassy appearance was discovered in Albert County, New Brunswick. Many disagree on who may have found the mineral first (various accounts credit its discovery to Gould Hoar, or John and Peter Duffy, or Abraham Gesner). It was mined throughout New Brunswick from about 1849 until 1884. When mixed with coal it became a valuable fuel source.

ALBERTOSAURUS

Often overshadowed by its distant relative, the Tyrannosaurus Rex, the Albertosaurus may have been smaller, but it was no less fearsome. Living some 76 to 74 million years ago during the late Cretaceous period, the Albertosaurus was about 9 m long, stood 3 m tall and weighed close to 2.7 tonnes; it was about half the size of the Tyrannosaurus Rex but lived 5 to 10 million years earlier. Albertosaurus had short, stubby arms;

9

long, powerful legs with clawed feet, and a long tail for balance and quick turns. Its teeth were able to punch through marrow, bone and tendon with great ease. Able to attain speeds of up to 40 km/h, the Albertosaurus may also have been one of the fastest predators of its day. Remains of Albertosaurus were discovered along the Red Deer River in Alberta in 1884 by Joseph Tyrrell, who was working for the Geological Survey of Canada. Harry Fairfield Osborn of the Natural History Museum in New York described the great lizard in 1905 (the same year that Alberta became a province), baptising it Albertosaurus or the Alberta lizard.

ALOUETTE

French for skylark, alouette is many things to many Canadians. To sports fans, the name of Montréal's Canadian Football League team is the Alouettes. Founded in 1946, the team gained immediate success but then drifted for years. It was renamed the Concordes in 1983 and folded in 1987, despite four Grey Cup titles. The Alouettes were resurrected in 1996 and won another league title in 2003. Alouette is also the name of a popular French-Canadian folk song that describes the preparation of a skylark for cooking. In Canada, the song is synonymous with Québec, but children sing it across the country. It was even once heard on an episode of *The Simpsons*. Alouette is also the name of the first Canadian-built satellite, launched into orbit from California on September 29, 1962, making Canada the third country to build and launch a satellite.

AMMOLITE

According to Blackfoot legend, a long, harsh winter once plagued its peoples. Their stores of food were nearly exhausted and could not be replenished. The great herds of bison had already moved on. Starved and cold, the Blackfoot turned to the heavens for assistance. The Great Goddess recognized their plight and, in a dream, she appeared to a young Blackfoot girl and told her to find a brilliantly coloured stone. The stone possessed magical qualities and when brought back to her tribe, the bison would return. The girl did as she was told and set off to find the stone. She wandered for days in the drifting snow but found nothing. Cold, she began looking for firewood when she suddenly heard singing from beneath a cottonwood tree. Curious, she began pawing at the snow and found the magnificent rainbow-coloured stone she had seen in her dreams. With the rock in her hand, she hurried back to her tribe. The next day, the Blackfoot were awakened by the sound of thundering hooves. The buffalo had returned. The stone had done its job and it became known as *Iniskim,* or the buffalo stone, and was used in buffalo-hunting ceremonies. The stone that the girl found may be one of the rarest gemstones in the world. In 1908, engineers with

11

the Canadian Geological Survey reported finding a brilliant gem in the bearspaw shale of southern Alberta, near Lethbridge. It was the fossilized shell of the ammonite, a hard-shelled squid that swarmed the waters of the vast, shallow sea that covered southern Alberta more than 65 million years ago. In 1967, a Calgary rock shop owner dubbed the stone ammolite, though it wouldn't be officially recognized as such until 1981. Also known as "grandmother of pearl," ammolite is extremely rare and highly prized for its use in both jewellery and holistic healing. It has been found in scattered locations across the globe, but its greatest concentration is in southern Alberta.

ANORAK

Ridiculed at length in one memorable episode of *Seinfeld*, the anorak may not be the most fashionable item in a closet, but it wasn't designed with style or aesthetics in mind. The puffy and somewhat chunky lines of the anorak do keep the cold out, which it was designed to do. As with many of Canada's now-common winter garments, the anorak was borrowed from the Inuit. Early Europeans, woefully unprepared for the arctic climate they encountered in North America, eagerly took up the garment and modified it. The anorak, originally made with waterproof sealskin and a hood, draws its name from the Inuit, *annoraqq*. Today, any heavy, hip-length jacket with a hood is referred to as an anorak. If you're shopping for an anorak in the United Kingdom, however, if be aware that there, anorak is also slang for a lover of all things computer.

ARBORITE

Arborite, like Formica, is a brand name that has come to be used to describe all sorts of plastic laminates. In 1942, at the Howard Smith Paper Mills in Cornwall, Ontario, researchers began experimenting with pulp resin in an attempt to develop a new decorative surface that could be used on desktops and countertops. Three years later, the first pressing of their melamine laminate was made. In January 1948, the Arborite Company was formed, and it began producing the thin laminates pasted onto particleboard seen so often on entertainment centres and computer desks today.

ARCTIC CHAR

The arctic char is the most northerly distributed freshwater fish (hence its name, although the etymology of char is unknown) and has been a part of the Inuit diet for centuries. Whether eaten raw, frozen, dried, smoked or cooked, arctic char is a nutritious fish, full of protein, vitamins and calcium. Its bones were used to make sewing needles, and its skins were used in the making of waterproof kayaking coats. It is the dominant species of the Arctic coast, but it wasn't until the 1940s that this northern species was caught commercially. Since then, arctic char has become prized at restaurants throughout Canada and the United States, with a flavour many describe as a cross between brook trout and salmon. Its flesh can be red, pink or white, though red demands the highest price.

BABY BONUS

Introduced in 1944, the Family Allowance Act was Canada's first universal welfare program. It originally provided monthly payments of $5 to $8 to all parents of children under 16; it's little surprise, then, that it became known as the baby bonus. Its introduction was meant to allay fears that six years of war would plunge the country into an economic depression, leaving parents unable to provide the basic needs for their children. The baby bonus was the beginning of social security in Canada, and it was quickly followed by unemployment insurance and a proposal for health insurance. It's known today as the Canada Child Tax Benefit, although only low-income families now qualify for it.

BALLICATTER

Ballicatter describes the ridges of ice formed on and around shores, rocks, vessels and wharves from waves and salt spray. Used most commonly in Newfoundland, ballicatter is an alteration of the word barricade and has been in use since the mid-19th century. It can also be used to describe frozen moisture around the nose and mouth.

BAKEAPPLES

Bakeapples, also known as baked-apple berries, as chicoute in Québec, as cloudberries in the United Kingdom, as hjortron in Sweden, as lakka in Finland and as molte in Norway, thrives in the bogs of coastal regions. They are a favourite of many northern cultures where humidity and relatively mild summer temperatures create the perfect conditions for the fruit to thrive. In Canada, they are found throughout Nova Scotia and Newfoundland. In late summer, when the berries are ready for picking, individuals of all ages come out to harvest the fruit. A relative of blackberries and raspberries, bakeapples are generally larger than both and bear an amber hue. They taste like the pulp of a roasted apple, a resemblance reflected in the fruit's name. Rich in flavonols and anthocyans—anti-oxidants that make berries among the most nutritious and healthy of all fruits—bakeapples are eaten either raw or cooked. They are used in recipes for everything from pies and toppings to jams and liqueurs.

BANGBELLY

It may not be the most popular dish in these Atkins-crazy days, but bangbelly has been a staple of Newfoundland cuisine for over a century. In its harsh Atlantic winters, you either ate large or you

16

spent your days shivering beneath your tuque. The word's origins are lost, but it was described in 1896 by a writer in the *Journal of American Folklore* as a "low and coarse word, denoting a boiled pudding consisting of flour, molasses, soda and not uncommonly seal-fat instead of suet." It sounds like pretty heavy, but definitely tasty stuff. Variously a pudding, cake or pancake, bangbelly was originally prepared by fishermen and trappers. They did not use molasses, preferring to mix their bangbellies with pork fat and drop them into pots of thick pea soup.

B

BEAVERTAILS

In 1978, bolstered by the modest success they'd had selling their pastries throughout the Ottawa Valley, Grant and Pam Hooker opened a permanent stand in Ottawa's Byward Market. They called their venture BeaverTails, and it wasn't long before their creation—a deep-fried, flat pastry shaped like a beavertail and topped with either sweet or savoury flavourings—became more than just a modest success. BeaverTails are now synonymous with Ottawa's outdoor festival, Winterlude, where they are sold in booths along the Rideau Canal. The snack's origins can be traced back to the days of the voyageurs, who often baked quick flatbreads over open fires. It has been adapted slightly, with help from a family recipe that traces its origins to a German pastry called *küchl* (German for little cake). BeaverTails are made from whole wheat flour, then rolled until they're about 30 cm long and 7.6 cm wide. Once cooked, they're topped with everything and anything from cinnamon sugar to maple butter to garlic butter to creamed cheese to salmon. Headquartered in Canada, the Hookers' company has gone global, with BeaverTails franchises located in the United States (one can be found at Walt Disney World in Florida), Costa Rica, Indonesia, the Philippines, Malaysia and Scotland.

BIRD COURSE

No, the term does not describe a class in ornithology. For generations of Canadian university students, a bird course was a gift from the academic gods, a gimme, a class beloved for its promise of an easy A. As with many slang terms, its origins are obscure, but it may have something to do with the slang connotations of the word "bird." In mid-19th century England, to give the bird was to express one's disapproval with a hiss that was meant to resemble the sound of a goose. It was a term of derision and dismissal.

BISCUIT

A euphemism for a hockey puck, biscuit and its cousin, the wafer, came into popular use during the 1940s. Sportswriters worried that they might be using the word puck a little too often and began creating their own words for the rubber disk. Biscuit caught on and is still used today.

BLACK BLIZZARD

Canadians entered the 1930s battered and weary. The Great Depression was still wreaking financial havoc, ravaging the human spirit and will. But for those who thought the dawning of a new decade would provide some relief, they were sorely mistaken. The Great Depression had only been a prelude. In the 1930s, the North American continent experienced one of its worst droughts in history. Between 1933 and 1937, the Prairie provinces received only 60 percent of their normal rainfall. Combined with poor agricultural practices, heat and high winds, the drought crippled the land, devastating and displacing millions of people throughout the United States and Canada. Livestock died in the millions and crops withered in arid fields. Over-ploughed and over-grazed, the parched prairie land was little more than dust. These conditions created a terrifying new phenomenon: the black blizzard, the severest kind of dust storm. When whipped into the air by the strong, dry winds that blew across the plains, black prairie soil rose up like a cloud, blocking out the sun and suffocating anything in its path. To many, it was the hand of God itself, descended from the heavens to bring about the end of the world. And that wouldn't be overstatement: some black blizzards were reported to be over 2400 km long, 1440 km wide and 3.2 km high. A quarter of a million people abandoned the prairies, and when the rains finally came, prairie farmers were left with ruined lives to rebuild and the searing image of the black blizzard.

B

BLOQUISTE

In 1990, the Meech Lake Accord, which would have recognized Québec as a distinct society, was defeated. Disappointed members of both the Progressive Conservative and Liberal parties, led by Lucien Bouchard, who had been federal Minister of the Environment, left their parties in disgust. Bouchard's band of disgruntled politicians formed the Bloc Québecois, a national political party that, like the Parti Québecois, would dedicate itself to Québec independence. Its members and supporters are sometimes called bloquistes, a derivation of the French word *bloc*, which means coalition. Although the party's support steadily declined during the 1990s, recent scandals involving the ruling Liberals have reinvigorated it.

BLOODY CAESAR

Also known as the Caesar, this drink may sound as if it has Roman origins, but in truth, they are more humble. The Bloody Caesar, which, like the Bloody Mary, incorporates tomato juice, vodka and Worcestershire sauce, was invented in Calgary in the late 1960s. Bartender Walter Chell had long tinkered with the drinks at the restaurant where he worked, wanting to create a savoury accompaniment that would complement the Italian fare that was heavy on tomatoes, spices and seafood.

One dish in particular captured his attention: the spaghetti vongele, essentially spaghetti with clams. For months, Chell worked on his concoction, until finally he pressed some clams into a nectar that he then mixed into a Bloody Mary. The drink was a success, with patrons claiming that it was fit for an emperor, and the Bloody Caesar was born. Chell's invention drew the attention of Mott's, a juice company based in California. At the time, Clamato was not as common on grocery store shelves as it is today, so to perfect its recipe, Mott's hired Chell to consult. Clamato became the mix of choice for bartenders all over the country who were looking to make Caesars. The Caesar continues to be popular with Canadians; in 2003, a survey found that more than 310 million Caesars had been sold in Canada alone, making it the country's most popular cocktail. It may have originated in a humble city on the prairies, but the Caesar is now truly worthy of its namesake.

BLUE NOSE

Blue nose is often used to describe people of a puritanical bent, but it also denotes a Nova Scotian. No one really seems to know why, as there are several different etymologies for the word. Bill Casselman, in his book *Casselman's Canadian Words*, writes that "nobody truly knows this [word's] origin," but he does offer a number of hypotheses. Could blue nose have been inspired by the chilled beaks of sailors returning from a journey into the Atlantic?

B

Or did it draw inspiration from the War of 1812, when a Nova Scotia privateer allegedly painted his cannon bright blue and earned a living harrying and attacking American ships, thus drawing their ire as well as the name The Blue Nose? Or does it have something to do with the *Blue Nose*, the schooner immortalized on the Canadian dime and which was originally built to win the International Prize? Whatever its origins, the word is most likely a source of pride for Nova Scotians. It confers ruggedness, hardiness and durability, qualities anyone living along the Atlantic must surely possess.

BOMBARDIER

Given our snowy climes, it's not surprising that it was a Canadian, James Armond Bombardier, who invented the snowmobile. Widely used today as a recreational vehicle, Bombardier's original snowmobile, created in the 1930s, seated 12 and was used to transport the ill and infirm through heavy snowfalls. It wasn't until the late 1950s, with the advent of lightweight engines, that his brainstorm's recreational potential was fully realized. With skis at the front and caterpillar tracks at the back, the yellow snowmobiles that became synonymous with his name made full use of his patented sprocket-wheel/track traction system. He had realized his boyhood dream to one day "build a little machine that glides over the snow." Today Bombardier Inc., the company that the man from a rural village in Québec started so many years ago, is world famous for its Ski-Doos, Sea-Doos and Lear jets.

B

THE BRIER

Football has its Grey Cup; hockey has its Stanley Cup. But for Canadian curlers, true greatness can only be attained at the Brier. Known today as the Nokia Brier, the Brier's roots go back to 1927. That year, Macdonald Tobacco sponsored a national men's curling competition and named it after one their most popular products—the Brier, a tobacco pipe made from the woody roots of a small Mediterranean shrub. The word brier came from *bruyere*, the French word for hearth, and it entered the Canadian consciousness, forever transcending its humble origins. When Macdonald Tobacco stopped sponsoring the event in 1979, Labatt retained the competition's moniker. In 2000, Nokia followed suit.

BRIN BAG

In Old English, *brinded* was used to describe fabric that was brown in colour. It evolved into brin, or strong, coarse-woven sacking. In other words, brin is burlap. Brin bags were used to store a wide variety of foodstuffs, including vegetables, animal feeds and breads. They were used to press blubber for its valuable oils. There was also the brin apron that stretched from the neck to the knees, and was worn when a floor needed a good scrubbing.

B

When a brin bag had outlived its intended purpose, enterprising Newfoundlanders found the fabric particularly useful in the hooking of rugs. The burlap was stretched tightly and nailed to a four-sided wooden frame. A design was then sketched onto the brin with charcoal. With a bent nail, strips of old clothing and fishing nets that had been dyed with vegetable dyes, spruce twigs and powders were then pulled through the burlap. It was arduous work, and some hooked rugs have as many as 200 loops per inch. The completed rugs were used to keep floors warm.

BUCK AND DOE

Stag parties have a long, storied tradition dating back to the days of ancient Sparta. On the night before his wedding, a Spartan would feast and drink with his friends for one last night of carousing before he settled into domesticity with his wife. At the end of the evening, if he and his friends were coherent enough, they would swear undying allegiance to one other. The stagette is a modern variation on the idea, as it seemed wholly unfair that women should be denied the same privilege. In rural Ontario, couples wanting neither the stag nor the stagette party united the two in what has become known as a buck and doe party (other names include a Jack and Jill and a stag and doe). The elements are the same, although there are some differences. A buck and doe is typically held in a hall, and guests are admitted only if they have previously bought a ticket from either the bride or the groom. Drinks are available for a small fee and to further entice guests to attend, prizes are awarded as well. Essentially a fund-raiser for the soon-to-be married couple, buck and doe parties have become increasingly popular throughout Canada and as far away as Alaska.

BUNNYHUG

Known as a kangaroo and a hoodie to some, the bunnyhug is what it's called in Saskatchewan. A bunnyhug is a hooded sweatshirt with a pocket in front to keep your hands warm, or store your keys or perhaps some tissue. Made of fabric that is fleecy on the inside, the bunnyhug has been described as a very warm item, particularly useful in warding off the freezing cold prairie winds of winter. Some even say that when you wear one, it feels a little like a bunny is giving you a hug. Is this the word's etymology? If so, then there must be some gargantuan rabbits in Saskatchewan.

BUSH PILOT

A bush pilot flies small aircraft over rugged, inaccessible terrain to remote areas. In Canada, the northern territories are the bush pilots' arena; for the remote communities they service, they are often the only connection to the outside world, and they bring with them mail, medicine and food supplies. Bush flying began after the First World War when Canadian combat pilots, enraptured with the idea of flight, sought avenues to put their skills to use. Bush piloting required a breed of individual with both piloting and mechanical skills. One of the earliest bush flights took place in 1920, when a fur buyer entered the Winnipeg offices of Canadian Aircraft and asked for a flight home to The Pas, hundreds of miles away with lakes, bushes, swamps and bogs lying in between. Today, the distance can be covered in 11 hours by automobile; in 1920, the terrain and distance made the journey extremely difficult. An intrepid pilot took the fur buyer home and showed that small planes could access remote areas of the North. Bush pilots continue to fly today, and although the planes they fly have improved vastly over the earliest bush planes, they are still participating in a Canadian tradition.

BUTTER TARTS

The butter tart has been a staple of the Canadian diet since its early days. Scottish immigrants coming to Nova Scotia brought with them a recipe for a particularly runny, gooey and delicious snack they called an Ecclefechan butter tart, named for a Scottish town that is also the birthplace of Thomas Carlyle. With its delicate crust and rich sweet centre, the dessert found a ready following; its ingredients were simple, incorporating items readily available in a settler cook's larder: butter, eggs, brown sugar and raisins. The Ecclefechan recipe differs in one aspect; it calls for the use of vinegar while its Canadian cousin does not. The debate continues about the origins of the butter tart as Canadians know and love it today. Some say that it might have been a take on the pecan pie of the American South (whose taste the butter tart resembles), or adapted from sugar pies or maple syrup pies. Regardless, the butter tart is firmly entrenched within the national identity, as Canadian as the beaver, the maple leaf and the Nanaimo bar.

THE BUTTERFLY

For a long time, hockey goalies were taught to stay on their feet or stack their pads to stop a puck. But in the 1960s and 1970s, two Canadian goalies revolutionized goaltending. Glenn Hall is widely credited with creating the butterfly, a style of goaltending so named for the way a goalie drops to the ice with both pads pushed laterally along the ice, splayed out like the wings of a butterfly. Tony Esposito used a sort of butterfly too, and both goalies had spectacular, Hall of Fame careers. But in its popularity lay its downfall, and while many goalies imitated the method, few knew how to use it properly. By the 1980s, goalies were once again advised to stand in their crease. But that was before Patrick Roy. Roy's recent success as a goalie using the butterfly has influenced generations of goaltenders in his native Québec. The province is often called a goaltending factory, with goalies such as Martin Brodeur, Patrick Lalime, and Marc Andre Fleury all finding success in the National Hockey League using the butterfly.

CABOTEUR

In the late 15th century, Giovanni Caboto, born near Naples, became John Cabot, an early explorer of North America who sailed under the English flag. Like the man who inspired its name, caboteur has gone through centuries of shifting origins. Originally a French word, caboteur was adopted by the English and then Canadians. The word is used throughout the world, although in Canada it very specifically describes a coastal trading ship or boat (or coaster, if you will) sailing the Gulf of Saint Lawrence and the Saint Lawrence River.

CALGARY REDEYE

Although redeye was originally used to describe any number of cheap whiskeys that Canadians might have brewed in their bathtubs or basement stills, in Calgary, redeye is now used to describe a combination of beer and tomato juice. No one knows who came up with the concoction, although perhaps someone looking to make a Bloody Mary had only beer to mix with the tomato juice, and a tasty treat was born. And while some may shudder at the thought of combining tomato juice with beer, the drink has passionate adherents who claim that a Calgary redeye approaches something akin to the sublime.

CALLIBOGUS

In the 18th century, many people found the local brews of Newfoundland not particularly strong and not very effective at producing inebriation. To spice up such concoctions as spruce beer (which has a low alcohol content), imbibers began mixing gin, rum and other liquors into their beer. Soon the mixtures contained more liquor than beer, and they came to be called callibogus. Callibogus has been consistently popular in Newfoundland for over two and a half centuries, and the combination of spruce beer, molasses and dark rum has become a drink in its own right.

CALUMET

Early French Canadians encountering the Mi'kmaq of Nova Scotia found that these Natives often carried a pipe festooned with beads, feathers and ribbons. To the French Canadians, the pipe looked very much like a beautiful foreign instrument. They called it the *chalumeau*—reed pipe. Later, they discovered that the reed pipe was not an instrument at all, but was a tobacco pipe of sacred and religious significance. To smoke from the pipe was to share in a communion with the animate powers of the world; it was used at the conclusion of peace treaties and at adoption ceremonies. Aboriginal ambassadors carried these pipes as proof of their identity. The pipe protected them from harm. *Chalumeau* was eventually anglicized into calumet.

CANADA DRY

In 1890, pharmacist and chemist John J. McLaughlin, a graduate of the University of Toronto, opened a small plant in Toronto to make soda water—a common mixer for fruit juices and extracts. In 1904, after years of work, McLaughlin unveiled a drink that would become known throughout the world as Canada Dry Pale Dry Ginger Ale. He wanted to duplicate the dry champagnes of France. McLaughlin revolutionized the carbonated beverage industry, taking it out of the corner drug store and to the public by mass bottling and distributing the drink in ballparks and at beaches. During Prohibition, Canada Dry's popularity soared, as many found the sweet, brown liquid the perfect mask for foul-tasting bathtub hooch. By 1938, Canada Dry was being produced in 14 countries and as far away as New Zealand. In 1986, Cadbury Schweppes, based in London, England, purchased Canada Dry and today, it is a part of Dr. Pepper/Seven Up Incorporated, itself the largest subsidiary of Cadbury Schweppes.

CANADA TEA

Also known as wintergreen (*Gaultheria procumbens*), Canada tea grows in the sandy and acid soils of eastern North America and has long been used in the folk medicine of the aboriginal tribes of North America. Early French explorers noticed how the Inuit of Labrador used the plant's glossy oval leaves and crimson fruits to treat a wide variety of ailments, including headaches, muscle aches and sore throats. The Delaware and Mohican used the plant to treat kidney disorders, while the Great Lakes and Eastern Woodlands tribes used poultices of Canada tea to treat arthritic and rheumatic pains. The Algonquin, Cherokee, Chippewa and Iroquois all used the plant as a herbal remedy. The explorers followed suit and took to steeping the leaves in boiling water. Today, herbalists use Canada tea to treat ailments because modern science has discovered that the plant produces a compound closely related to aspirin. It must be used in moderation. In high doses, it can aggravate both the stomach and the kidney.

CANADA THISTLE

Canada thistle (*Cirsium arvense*) is pretty notorious, even for a weed. Aggressive and hardy, Canada thistle is the bane of many a farmer's and gardener's existence, although it didn't originate in Canada at all. It was probably introduced into North America in the early 17th century, a contaminant in the crop seeds brought over by the settlers of New France. The weed took root and became so prevalent throughout eastern Canada

C

that aboriginal tribes had enough time to actually develop medicinal uses for the plant, using it to treat a wide range of stomach illnesses before the it spread throughout the continent. It's unknown how the thistle came to be named after Canada.

CANADARM

In 1981, the American space shuttle *Columbia* rocketed into orbit, bearing with it the Shuttle Remote Manipulator System. The SRMS is known more familiarly as the Canadarm, Canada's first contribution to NASA's space shuttle program. NASA was so impressed with the Canadarm's performance that it has, over the years, ordered four of them, resulting in $900 million in export sales. The Canadarm was the brainchild of MD Robotics, which had been hired by the National Research Council of Canada. The Canadarm's main duty is to place satellites into orbit and retrieve them for any necessary repairs. Most notably, it played a crucial role in the repair of NASA's Hubble Space Telescope, which could have been a costly and crippling embarrassment for the beleaguered agency. It is currently being used to help build the International Space Station.

CANADIAN WHISKEY

Canadian whiskey trails only vodka in distilled spirits consumed in the United States, accounting for 11.5 percent of the market. Although Canadian whiskey is commonly called rye, the latter is a bit of a misnomer. Canadian whiskey is typically a blend of corn, rye and barley, with corn being the principle ingredient. However, rye, even in the smallest amounts, can influence the flavour of the drink, giving it a spicy flavour. Canadian whiskey has its roots in the 19th century, when rum, which was easily and widely available, was mixed with high wine, a whiskey spirit made from grains, to add flavour. It was also widely used in trade with aboriginals, who found the "fire-water" of the Europeans addictive as well as intoxicating. Canadian whiskey's popularity south of the border can be directly attributed to American Prohibition in the 1920s. In 1924, two-thirds of whiskey imported into the United States came from Canadian distilleries, which had built factories all along the Great Lakes near Detroit to serve the American market. Seagram's and Hiram Walker both made fortunes from this illicit trade. After Prohibition was repealed, Canadian whiskey continued to be popular as American distillers scrambled to rebuild their dismantled operations.

CANDU REACTOR

Designed and developed in the late 1950s through a cooperative effort between the Canadian government and the private sector, the CANDU nuclear reactor is a pressurized heavy water, natural uranium power reactor. It was first used in 1962, at Rolphton, Ontario, and began providing power to thousands of homes and families. Using technology that had been developed for the construction of the atomic bomb, Canadian scientists hoped that they had created something that could bring safe and inexpensive power to the world. Standing for Canada Deuterium Uranium and not the can-do attitude of the researchers and scientists who built it, the CANDU reactor had many advantages over other nuclear generators. Running on unenriched uranium, it could be operated without expensive fuel enrichment facilities, and it needed no large pressure vessels. It was highly efficient too, even if it did use the purest and most expensive grade of heavy water ever developed. Unfortunately, its strengths turned out to be weaknesses, and while the CANDU reactor continues to be sold across the globe, many people see these sales as a potential threat to world security. Theoretically, the reactor and its unenriched uranium fuel could be used to produce plutonium for nuclear weapons. Still, in 1987, the CANDU reactor was named one of the top 10 Canadian engineering achievements on a list that included the CN Tower, the Bombardier snowmobile and the St. Lawrence Seaway.

CANOLA
Known for its brilliant yellow flowers that can make a field look like a bright golden carpet, canola is a modified member of the rapeseed

family. Before the Second World War, rapeseed oil was used commonly in kitchens and as an engine lubricant. In Asia, it has been used as a cooking oil for over 4000 years. But following the Second World War, concerns were raised about the high levels of both erucic acid and glucosinates in rapeseed oil. Heart disease was blamed on erucic acid, while glucosinate proved toxic to animals when it began to break down. Canadian planters began experimenting with the rapeseed to create a "double-low" variety: low in erucic acid and low in glucosinates. In 1974, Baldur Stefansson at the University of Manitoba crossbred the first variety, which he called Tower. In 1979, the name was changed to canola by the Western Canadian Oilseed Crushers Association, shorthand for Canadian oil low acid. Its health claims are disputed by conspiracy-minded theorists, who believe Canada is on a mission to grow wealthy off the peddling of its "industrial oil." Detractors cite canola's associations with the rapeseed, which is erroneously believed to have been used in the manufacture of mustard gas, and the incorrect belief that canola was genetically engineered. Canola has even somehow managed to be blamed for mad cow disease. Regardless, canola oil's popularity is growing, and Canada now accounts for 15 percent of the world's production.

CANUCK

Originally used by northeastern Americans as a derogatory term for French Canadians following the American Revolution, Canuck has become a name of pride for both francophones and anglophones, although foreigners are advised not to use the word liberally. The origins of Canuck are not clear, and there are many theories about the word's origins. One suggests that it originated from a combination of the French expression *quelle canule* and cold weather. In 1776, during a siege on Québec, American troops, under the command of Benedict Arnold, heard *quelle canule* repeated often among the French enemy, so they began repeating it, too. But unaccustomed to the cold, the Americans couldn't stop shivering when they spoke, and they ended their *canules* with a "k" sound. Another theory offers the idea that it may have originated with German mercenaries captured at Saratoga from Burgoyne's army. When given the opportunity to return to Canada, they allegedly replied, "Nien! Nien! Genug vun Kanada." Unsure of what they said, their captors instead took to repeating "Genug vun Kanada" over and over again, until they decided finally to drop the "vun." Genug Kanada could have become Canuck. Still another theory says that Canuck is derived from the Iroquoian word for hut: *kanuscha.* Or maybe it came from *Connaught*, a popular Irish surname that early French Canadians mistook for a nickname for

Irish Canadians. Regardless, the word Canuck appears as early as the mid-19th century. Johnny Canuck appeared shortly thereafter and became as synonymous with Canada as John Bull with Britain and Uncle Sam with the United States. Today, it is more familiarly associated with the perennially disappointing Vancouver Canucks hockey team of the NHL and with the very brief period when the Crazy Canucks of Canada competed with the likes of Austria and Germany for skiing supremacy.

CAPLIN

Newfoundland has always been closely tied to the ocean and has a proud fishing heritage. It was the abundant cod that brought fishermen from France, England and Spain to the area in the 16th century. The silvery caplin (*Mallotus villosus*) may be small—no more than 17–19 cm long—but they loom large in the Newfoundland consciousness. The word, derived from the French word *capelan*, meaning "codfish," has been in use since the early 17th century. A close relative of freshwater smelt, caplin is one of the most important forage species in the Northwest Atlantic. Preying upon plankton, caplin is a favoured prey of flounder, whales, seals and cod. Recognizing this relationship, early Newfoundland fishermen looked forward each year to early summer, when schools of caplin would come ashore during the caplin scull to breed. There

C

was a time when entire villages would turn out for the caplin scull. Armed with buckets and dip nets, the people gathered up the spawning caplin for use not just as bait for cod, but as fertilizers for gardens, as feed for sled dogs and, when dried and salted, as a tasty and welcome alternative to salt beef. The caplin scull no longer inspires the fervour and excitement as it once did, and it's a loss that many Newfoundlanders still lament.

CARIBOU

The caribou is a kind of deer native to northern Canada's tundra regions. It has large antlers that are present in both sexes, though female antlers are significantly smaller and simpler. In Europe, caribou are known as reindeer, the very same that pull Santa's sleigh every Christmas Eve. For centuries, the caribou has played a prominent role in the aboriginal cultures of Canada's north as a source of food, fuel and clothing in an environment sorely lacking all three. Its name is a corruption of the Mi'kmaq word *xalibu* or *xalipu*, meaning "one who paws," and has been in use since the mid-17th century. According to Bill Casselman, aboriginals often observed the *xalibu* pawing its way through the snow to get to the grass below. The word has new meaning in Québec, where caribou has become the name of a particularly potent and mind-numbing alcoholic drink. Also known as caribou juice, caribou is made of one part red wine and six parts grain alcohol. One variation substitutes dandelion wine for the red wine and gin for the grain alcohol.

CATTALO

The Boyds of Bobcageyon, Ontario, were an entre-preneurial lot. In 1844, Mossom Boyd built Bobcageyon's first sawmill and was soon running the third largest lumber operation in Ontario. When Boyd died in 1883, it was turned over to his two sons, Mossom Martin and Willie. They formed the MM Boyd Lumber Company and expanded their timber limits from Ontario into Québec and as far away as the Northwest Territories and British Columbia. Mossom Martin had other interests as well. Cattle brought into the West from Eastern Canada were ill equipped to deal with the extremes of the prairie climates. Settlers there quickly learned that cattle from the western United States, like the bison that once roamed the vast plains of North America in great numbers, were hardier and sturdier creatures, better adapted to long, harsh winters. It seemed that some of these durable creatures were the progeny of natu-ral crossbreeding between bison and cattle. By 1885, ranchers were deliberately mating the two. In 1894, Mossom Martin began his own cross-breeding program and called his resultant hybrid the cattalo, a cross of the words cattle and buffalo. None of his animals produced offspring, as the males were usually sterile while the females pos-sessed underdeveloped reproductive organs. Nor

C

did they possess any pronounced advantage in growth or carcass performance. Yet, others picked up the work he began. Agriculture Canada experimented with the breed from 1916 until 1965. Researchers at the University of Guelph produced some cattalo in the 1970s for a study on the genetic aspects of crossbreeding. Cattalo meat is said to be low in both fat and cholesterol, but higher in protein and iron. In the United States, the hybrid is known as the beefalo.

CHEECHAKO

A word that has its origins in both the Yukon and Alaska, cheechako is a combination of two Indian words: the Chinook word *chee*, meaning "new and fresh," and the Nootka word, *chako*, meaning "to approach or to come." Used as long ago as the early 19th century by traders of the Hudson's Bay Company, cheechako was used to describe immigrants newly arrived to the Yukon. They might also have been called Outsiders. It has a slightly pejorative meaning and is used in much the same way as city slicker, tenderfoot and greenhorn are. *Ballads of Cheechako* was a poem written in the early 20th century by Robert W. Service.

CHIMO

First recorded in 1748, although probably much older, chimo is the Inuit equivalent of hello or greetings. It also means friendship. According to some accounts, when meeting in the North, people would rub their chests in a circular motion and then say, "Chimo?" to which the other person would respond in kind. In that context, chimo was being used to ask, "Are you friendly?"

C

CHINOOK

A Chinook is a warm, dry easterly wind that sweeps down the eastern slopes of the Rocky Mountains and often brings a welcome, though all too brief, respite from the polar temperatures of a long winter. It is aptly described in this passage from a 1900 edition of the *Calgary Weekly Herald*:
"Those who have not the warm, invigorating Chinook winds of this country, cannot well comprehend what a blessing they are. The icy clutch of winter is lessened, the earth throws off its winding sheet of snow. Humanity ventures forth to inhale the balmy spring-like air. Animated nature rejoices."
A Chinook can cause great changes in weather; one dramatic transformation occurred in Calgary on January 11, 1983, when the temperature rose by 30 degrees, from −17° C to +13° C, in four hours. Also known as a snow-eater, a Chinook thaws snowbanks and can melt as much as 2.5 cm of ice from frozen ponds and lakes in just one hour. Its name is taken from a Pacific Northwest Coast tribe that once lived along the banks of the lower Columbia River. Although the Chinook has been blamed recently on the high incidence of

migraines and allergies among those living in its path, most people welcome its arrival and speak warmly of the wind that has "chinooked them."

C

CHINOOK JARGON

The early 19th century in British Columbia was the heyday of Chinook Jargon, the trade language of the Pacific Northwest. The region was a melting pot, with traders from France and England working closely with aboriginals such as the Salish and the Nootka. It's not surprising that they created their own common, yet multicultural, mosaic of a language. English fur traders were known as *kin chotsch-men*, or King George Men. The French were *passioks*, a word meaning "blanket-men," while Americans were called *Boston-men*. Many Chinook Jargon words are still in use in western Canada, and it is still spoken as a first language among some residents of Oregon. Linguists believe that a trade language, the forerunner of Chinook Jargon, existed before the late 17th century.

CIPAILLE

A layered meat pie, the cipaille is a traditional French Canadian dish that was cited at least as early as 1747, when it appeared in a cookbook. A typical cipaille consists of three layers of meat, spices and potato, separated by pastry, baked in a cast-iron pot. At one time, there may have been as many as six layers, which led to the name, *six-pâtes*, and the eventual corruption of that word into cipaille or cipâte. In Ontario, the dish is known as sea pie, an anglicized pronunciation of the French word.

C

COADY

Popular in Newfoundland, especially to pour over boiled pudding, coady is a sweet sauce of boiled molasses mixed with butter. It has also been made with milk, sugar and vinegar and thickened with cornstarch. According to Bill Casselman, the word may have been derived from *coaty* or *coatie*, a coating on food.

COHO SALMON

Also known as silver salmon, hooknose and sea trout, the Coho salmon (*Oncorhynchus kisutch*) is native to the Pacific coast of Canada and has long been part of the diet of aboriginals such as the Salish. Its name is an alteration of the Salish word *cohose*, and so important was this fish to Salish society that the month of September was called *chen'thaw'en*, or the time of the Coho. The Coho is a small fish, with an average weight of 2.3–2.7 kg, and though it is native to the north Pacific, it has been introduced with great success into the Great Lakes. The Coho is a dark metallic blue colour, with tints of green on its back and upper sides.

COPY

With the popularity of extreme sports these days, one wonders why copy, a game and pastime popular in Newfoundland, has yet to acquire the same popularity as street luging or base jumping. Originating in the late 19th century, copy draws its name from the childhood game of follow or copy the leader. Usually played in spring, copy began when children, in imitation of sealers, began jumping from one piece of floating ice to another. Not exactly the safest of pastimes, the game courted danger, as not every ice pan was buoyant enough to support the weight of the jumpers. Leaping from one large floe of ice to another was considered too safe and not in keeping with the spirit of copying. The term now applies to anyone crossing any pan of ice, even if there is no game involved. But there are days in spring when people can be heard fondly recalling, as they did to the *Canadian Journal of Linguistics* in 1964, that "we were so busy catching tomcods, copying pans in the spring that we didn't have time to chase all our vitamins" and that "the minute school was out we ran helter-skelter to one of the coves to copy pans."

COULEE

Though the word has spread to the south and is used throughout the western United States, coulee's origins lie in the French Canadian language.

Meaning "a deep gulch or ravine," usually with inclined sides and dry in the summer, coulee is a French Canadian word whose origins lie in the French verb *courer*, meaning "to run or to flow."

C

CRETONS

Not to be confused with a cretin, cretons is a pâté-like, highly seasoned pork spread popular through-out Québec. Spread on toast, cretons is a favourite breakfast item. It has its origins in medieval France and a coarse pâté of ground pork and pork fat. Creton was originally used in Old French to describe a piece of fried pork fat.

DAMPER DOGS

A sort of pancake, damper dogs (other names include damper boy, damper cake and damper devil) are small pieces of dough that have been fried atop a stove's damper, an adjustable plate used to control the draft on a woodstove or coalstove. Harold Horwood recalled in his 1969 book, *Newfoundland*, that his grandmother often made damper dogs to tide her grandchildren over until she could make a new batch of bread.

DEKE

Deke, as both a verb and noun, first entered Canadian English usage in the 1960s. An abbreviation of the word decoy, deke was used to describe a fake or feint used to fool a defender or a goalie on an opposing hockey team. The word was just too good to be limited to the sport of ice hockey and can now be employed in a variety of contexts, including deking your way out of something you don't want to do.

DÉPANNEUR

In France, a dépanneur is usually a repairman who specializes in electronics or automobiles, or someone who helps you out of a tough spot. It's this philanthropic flavour of the word that's at the root of the Québecois version of the word. In Québec, a dépanneur is not a repairman; it's not a man at all. The dépanneur is a convenience store, usually open from 7:00 in the morning until 11:00 at night, able to provide all sorts of items and typically family owned and operated. In previous decades, dépanneurs were the only stores in the province permitted to sell beer and other alcoholic beverages. The word was once used strictly by francophones, although it is now a part of Québecois English as well. It's also known as the dep.

DIGBY CHICKEN

The word gained some notoriety in 2001 when it tripped up mathematics student Shannon Patrick Sullivan of Memorial University of Newfoundland on the Canadian edition of *Who Wants to be a Millionaire?* The question was worth $16,000, but Sullivan guessed incorrectly that in Nova Scotia, digby chicken refers to smoked lobster. Nova Scotians know that digby chicken refers to smoked and salted herring. The tiny fish are a popular snack in Digby, the fishing port from which it draws its name. Digby itself was named for Admiral Robert Digby, who brought Loyalists from America to Nova Scotia aboard the H.M.S. *Atlanta* in 1783.

DULSE

Originally popular in Ireland, the purply-red seaweed known as dulse was also found to thrive along the North Atlantic coast of Canada. Settlers of New Brunswick found the edible seaweed as tasty and appetizing as it had been in Europe, and it is now commonly used throughout the Maritimes as a condiment in both soups and stews. Found on rocks, fronds of dulse can vary in colour, from a pink to purple, and is picked by hand between the months of June and September. The fronds are spread on netting to dry, for eager and health-conscious consumers to eat either as is (pan frying them is common, as is baking them in the oven) or to add to doughs, sandwiches and chowders. High in vitamins, potassium and fluoride, dulse is treasured throughout Canada for both its taste and nutrition. Nova Scotia markets its dulse as sea parsley. The word dulse itself is Gaelic in origin; its root word is *duileask*, which means, appropriately, "sea bits."

E

EAGER BEAVER

The beaver, industrious and hard-working, is our national animal, a source of pride and patriotism. Coined by the Canadian army in the mid-20th century, eager beaver is an offshoot of other expressions, such as "busy as a beaver," that play off the beaver's hardy reputation. Eager beaver is commonly used as a term of derision, applied to anyone demonstrating excessive zeal or enthusiasm.

EH

Perhaps no word is considered as distinctly Canadian as eh. The word has been in use for well over 1000 years, with roots in both Latin, Old English and Middle English. In Latin, it was derived from the word *interiectio*, which means "something thrown in between." In Middle English, the word was *ey*, an interjection common in Geoffrey Chaucer's *Canterbury Tales*. Even then, the word was considered slang, and little has changed over the centuries. In Canada, eh is used at the end of a statement, basically turning the statement into a rhetorical question and tacitly assuming the other person's agreement—"It's cold in Canada, eh? I sure could go for a beer, eh?" and so forth. It's not exactly clear how the expression became so popular in Canada and how it became so closely identified with the country. Even in 1959, the *Journal of Canadian Linguistic Association* was reporting that "eh is so exclusively a Canadian feature that immigration officials use it as an identifying clue."

ERMITE CHEESE

First produced by the monks of Saint-Benoît Abbey in eastern Québec in 1943 with the opening of the Fromagerie de L'Abbaye, ermite is a semi-soft, blue cheese. Rindless with a bluish vein and an aroma resembling mushrooms, ermite was named after the French word *l'ermite*, meaning "hermit." The Saint-Benoît Abbey is a popular Roman Catholic retreat.

ESKIMO

For years, the native inhabitants of the Arctic and subarctic regions of North American and Siberia were known collectively as the Eskimo. And, for years, people believed that the term was derived from the Algonquin word for "eater of raw flesh." Living in a harsh environment with few trees and resources for cooking fuel, the northern Natives did often eat their meat raw, a habit that appalled the supposedly more civilized and more cultured European explorers. But it was the Europeans who suffered from scurvy in great numbers, while the Eskimos thrived and, until recently, suffered little from typically Western ailments such as heart disease. In the 1970s, the term Eskimo was replaced with Inuit in Canadian governmental and scientific publications. In recent years, however, linguists have begun to argue that the basis for the word Eskimo may not have been "eater of raw flesh" at all, but may, in fact, have come from a Montagnais word that described the lacing of a snowshoe. The matter remains unsettled. It should be noted that the word that has come to replace Eskimo, Inuit, refers only to the Inuit-speaking people of northern Canada and some parts of Greenland. The northern Indians of Alaska and Arctic Siberia are known, respectively, as the *Inupiaq* and the *Yupik*.

FIDDLEHEADS

Popular in spring throughout Québec and the Maritimes, fiddleheads are the croziers or tightly curled, young and edible tips of the ostrich fern. When boiled or steamed, fiddleheads lose their natural bitter taste and acquire a flavour that many say is uniquely earthy, grassy and nutty, similar only to the flavour of cooked asparagus or artichoke. Rich in vitamins A and C, fiddleheads have been a food staple for centuries, figuring prominently in the diets of early Natives, especially New Brunswick's Maliseet. Maliseet clothing, canoes and wigwams were often decorated with a fiddlehead motif, reflecting its prominence in Maliseet culture. It was from the Natives that early French explorers learned of the fiddlehead. It acquired its name from English traders and trappers, who thought that the spiral shape of the frond resembled the scroll found at the head of a violin or fiddle. In other parts of the country, fiddleheads are available fresh for a short time in June and frozen year-round.

FIRST NATIONS

The term First Nations was popularized in the 1970s as a welcome alternative to the term Indian, which many Canadians aboriginals found insulting and offensive (it is a term based, after all, on an assumption made by Christopher Columbus). First Nations has come to refer to the tribes of six major cultural regions across Canada: the Woodland First Nations, the Iroquois First Nations, the Plains First Nations, the Plateau First Nations, the First Nations of the Pacific Coast and the First Nations of the Mackenzie and Yukon River basins.

F

FIVE-HOLE

According to hockey tradition, there are five holes that a goalie typically leaves exposed. The one-hole is found in the upper left corner, the two-hole in the upper right, the three-hole in the lower left and the four-hole in the lower right. To increase the area of the net that the goalie covers, he or she typically crouches, with the legs splayed out. The space thus created between the legs is referred to as the five-hole. People rarely talk about the other holes, but to be beaten through the five-hole is a great source of embarrassment for a goalie. Some hockey historians claim that the five-hole's origins may also lie in the Roman numeral for five: V. When a goalie is in his crouch, the area between his legs looks similar to an inverted V.

FOG-EATER

The term has many definitions. In the United States, a fog-eater is a coastal inhabitant. For railwaymen, the fog-eater is an engineer. But in most ocean regions, a fog-eater, a term that has been in use since at least the 19th century by seamen and those accustomed to fog, refers to either a rainbow or a white bow in the clouds seen in heavy fog that usually precedes the fog's lifting. In Canada's North, the term is used frequently, a remnant of the first European settlers, and it doesn't take great imagination to realize the term's etymology.

FOUR-POINTER

During the 1690s, French fur traders were scouring the North American wilderness for the beaver and mink furs so popular in Europe. They also relied heavily upon aboriginal tribes for pelts, and traded goods such as alcohol, trinkets and blankets for the pelts. A four-pointer was a large, thick and heavy blanket, durable and compact enough to fight back the Canadian cold. Noted for its warmth and versatility, this blanket could be adapted for use as clothing. Trade blankets were made under a point system, a point being a unit of measurement. One-pointers were the smallest, also called "cradle blankets." The largest were five-pointers, although French traders were outfitted most often with the four-pointer.

FOX 40

To referees everywhere, the Fox 40 was and is a lifesaver. The Fox 40 is a whistle, invented and developed by Canadian referee Ron Foxcroft in the late 1980s. Prior to the Fox 40, most whistles used by referees in leagues such as the National Basketball Association and the National Hockey League were cork-pea whistles. They usually did their job, but cork-pea whistles are notoriously temperamental and finicky. If blown too hard, they make no sound. If they get dirty or wet, they make no sound. If a crowd is particularly loud, and the cork-pea whistle does work, no one can hear its feeble tone. And if a whistle makes no sound or is inaudible when it does, how is a referee to do his job? Foxcroft finally decided to make a change after the 1976 Montréal Olympics. Before a crowd of 18,000 fans gathered to watch the basketball final game between the United States and Yugoslavia, Foxcroft saw a Yugoslav player elbow an American player. He blew his whistle. There was no sound. Play went on, and Foxcroft found himself the object of a chorus of boos and hisses. After working on 14 prototypes, Foxcroft finally perfected his pea-less whistle, which had no moving parts to malfunction and a loud, ear-splitting tone that could be heard above the rowdiest of crowds. The Fox 40, named after Foxcroft and for the age he was on the day he patented his invention, was used professionally for the first time at the

Pan-Am Games in Indianapolis, Indiana, in 1987. Its success and efficiency had the Indianapolis Police Department asking for Fox 40 whistles. In 1990, the whistle was being used by the National Basketball Association, the National Collegiate Athletic Association and the Canadian Football League. It has been used in the World Cup of soccer. The Fox 40 may just very well be the referee's new best friend.

FRANCOPHONE, ALLOPHONE, ANGLOPHONE

Francophone, allophone and anglophone are words that have migrated to Canadian English from Québecois French. These words reflect Canada's cultural diversity, its aboriginal heritage and its two official languages. A francophone is one who claims French as a mother tongue and primary language; an anglophone claims English as a mother tongue; and an allophone is usually an immigrant or an aboriginal person whose native tongue is something other than English or French. In 2001, the Canada Census found that 59.1% of Canadians are anglophones, 22.9% are francophones, and 18% are allophones. Chinese is the third most common language spoken in Canada.

FRAZIL

Derived from the French word *frasil*, frazil is a French Canadian term for fine individual ice crystals that appear either as spicules (long and needle-like splinters of ice) or as plates suspended in water. Frazil is often found in waters too turbulent for pack ice to form and in icebanks along shorelines. *Frasil* is French for cinder, which French Canadians felt the ice resembled. The term has been in use since the late 19th century.

G

GARBURATOR

Although the origins of this word are lost (linguists believe that it may have once been a Canadian trade name for a garbage disposal unit—probably a hybrid of garbage and incinerator), garburator has become the Canadian term to describe an under-the-sink garbage disposal unit. First invented by Racine architect John W. Hammes in 1927, the garburator gained widespread popularity and acclaim in the 1970s and 1980s. Environmental concerns curbed its use for a while, but it remains a staple of Canadian kitchens everywhere, ready to consume all food waste and mangle the occasional stray utensil.

GASPEREAU

In Nova Scotia, there is a town called Gaspereau, a Gaspereau Valley, a Gaspereau Mountain and a Gaspereau River. In a province so closely tied with the ocean and its bounty, it's not surprising that so many places have been named after a fish. Known to the English as alewife, gaspereau is an Acadian French word for a small, herring-like fish that has been a staple of Nova Scotia's economy since its earliest days. Gaspereau is fished in spring with traps, gill nets and dip nets when it enters freshwater rivers such as the Saint John in New Brunswick and the Gaspereau in Nova Scotia to spawn, and is used as bait in lobster and snow crab traps. It can also be found on local menus fresh, dried, smoked or salted, its roe is sold as a delicacy and it is used in the making of pet foods. No wonder that the versatile fish, also known as kiack in Nova Scotia, is in danger of being overfished. In 1958, North Atlantic fisheries caught 75 million pounds of gaspereau. In recent years, the catch has dropped to less than 5 million.

GAUNCH, GINCH, GONCH or GITCH

Why are there so many different terms for underwear in Canada? It's a mystery, although gaunch is a term that appears to be specific to British Columbia and Alberta while gitch seems to be a favourite among Ontarians. No one knows why, but perhaps the difference may be tied to western alienation; Ontario has its term, so the West must have its own. It's important to note that the terms don't just describe any sort of undergarment; to qualify as a gaunch, ginch, gonch or gitch, an undergarment must be a little worn, dirty and malodorous.

GOOEYDUCK

Slang for geoduck, gooeyduck might have come about because people couldn't pronounce the word correctly. The geo in the word isn't pronounced like the geo in geography, but like the slang—gooey. The pronunciation of the word is based in Nisqually and Chinook Jargon, which are old trader languages of southern British Columbia. The gooeyduck is the largest burrowing clam in the world. It is found deep beneath the sands of ocean beaches along British Columbia's coast. The Nisqually tribe found the clam particularly tasty but difficult to harvest. They called it the *go-duk*, meaning "dig-deep." The name carried over into English, and traders found the clam quite appetizing as well. Harvesting the geoduck is more than a little tricky, but given that the geoduck can live for as long as 146 years, harvesters have time on their side.

GOPHER
When French explorers arrived in North America, they noticed a short-tailed, burrowing rodent that plagued crops. They discovered that the animal lived beneath the ground in a honeycomb-like network of carefully constructed tunnels. To this animal with its cute, fur-lined cheeks, French explorers gave the name *gaufre gris*. In French, *gaufre* means "honeycomb." English settlers adopted the word but not the spelling.

GREY CUP
The Grey Cup, which has been associated with Canadian football excellence for almost a century,

was intended to be a trophy for Canada's senior amateur hockey champion. Unfortunately, Governor General Lord Albert Henry Earl Grey was unable to bequeath his gift; in 1910, banking mogul Sir Hugh Andrew Montagu Allan donated his own championship hockey trophy, the Allan Cup, making Lord Grey's cup unnecessary. Undaunted, Lord Grey decided to donate the trophy to the champions of amateur football. The Grey Cup was contested for years by amateur Canadian teams, but in 1958, professional football emerged in Canada with the creation of the Canadian Football League, and the Grey Cup has been coveted by CFL teams ever since.

GRITS

Grits, the nickname for members of the Liberal Party and not the food so popular in the American south, was first popularized in the mid-19th century. Editor and political reformer George Brown used the phrase "Clear Grit" often to describe members of his wing of the Reform party, a group of rural Presbyterian and Methodist farmers unhappy with the ruling political parties. Clear Grit was a highly symbolic term. In the United States, someone having clear grit was said to be unflinching and obstinate, qualities Brown believed reformers needed to possess, but it also referred to the first-grade sand that Scottish stonemasons of Upper Canada used in making mortar. After Confederation, Brown's Reform party disappeared; the Liberal Party, which also represented disenchanted rural Protestant farmers, was given the mantle instead.

GST

Although many initially considered GST an acronym for the Gouge and Screw Tax, GST is really an acronym for the Goods and Services Tax. In 1989, Brian Mulroney and his Progressive Conservative government proposed the creation of a national sales tax and though opposition was fierce, it came into being on January 1, 1991. The tax, a 7 percent charge on goods and services, ruined the Progressive Conservative Party, and in 1993, Jean Chretien and the Liberal Party were elected with a strong majority. Chretien's promise to repeal the GST never happened because the much-maligned tax was a great source of federal revenue. Canadians today have accepted the GST, although people in Alberta long for the days when they paid no taxes at all on any goods and services—Alberta is the only province in Canada without a provincial sales tax.

GTA

GTA is an acronym used for decades to describe the Greater Toronto Area. Taken together, the GTA and Toronto make up the largest metropolitan area in Canada and fourth largest in North America, with a population of over 5 million. The GTA includes cities such as Barrie, Burlington and Mississauga and towns such as Markham and Oakville. The area is so large that it uses six distinct area codes, which has led to the creation of an area code aristocracy. The 416s are for those living in Toronto and are the most coveted; everything outside is known as The 905s, even though there are four other area codes within the GTA.

G

H

HABS

Habs is the nickname for one of Québec's most beloved institutions, the Montréal Canadiens, and is short for *habitants*, the name given to early French settlers. The term was at one time pejorative, akin to redneck or yokel, and came to include not just a farmer, but anyone from rural Québec. The H and the C that form the Montréal Canadiens' logo actually stand for "Club de Hockey Canadien," but in 1924, American reporter Tex Rickard was mistakenly told that the H stood for habitants and the team's French farmer hockey players. Rickard passed the information on, and the name stuck.

HAT TRICK

Although the hat trick is strongly associated with scoring three goals in a hockey game (at which point fans throw their hats and caps onto the ice), its origins rest not in hockey, but in cricket. Dating back to the late 1800s, a hat trick was achieved when a bowler took three wickets off with three successive balls, a rare and celebrated feat. The bowler was usually given a hat as a reward for his efforts, although some say the term may have originated with the tradition of the bowler passing his cap through the crowd to collect tips after completing a hat trick. It is believed that hockey's version of the hat trick may have started in the 1940s, when a Toronto hat maker promised free hats to any player scoring three goals in a game. The first hat trick in hockey history has been lost to time, although some claim that Joe Malone was the first to score three goals in a game. Wayne Gretzky owns the record for most hat tricks with 50. A hat trick is increasingly rare in the goal-stingy NHL of today, and rarer still is the natural hat trick: three consecutive goals scored by one player.

HIGH MUCKAMUCK

In Chinook Jargon, *hyas muckamuck* meant "big food" and "plenty to eat." It could also be used to describe a feast. Guests often found the local aristocracy, who were invited to sit at the head table, arrogant and overbearing, and soon the corrupted term high muckamuck entered Canadian English slang to describe such folk. A derogatory term, it was applied to any important yet overbearing person and was first cited in 1856.

HOCKEY

As Canada's national sport and favourite pastime, hockey inspires much debate and passion;

the word itself inspires almost as much as the game. It may have been a derivation of the word hurley. It may have been coined in Halifax, Nova Scotia, in the 1860s. Or it may have been derived from the French word *hoquet* meaning "a shepherd's crooked staff or stick." It spread eastward from the Maritimes, through to Québec and Ontario. By the end of the 19th century, the game had become a national phenomenon, and hockey, regardless of its origins, had become shorthand for Canadian nationality and pride, as well as a boon for beer manufacturers such as Labatt and Molson.

HOOTCH

Hootch is fairly common throughout Canada and is used to describe any kind of homebrew liquor. The word originated in the Yukon and British Columbia and was borrowed from the Tlingit word, *khutsnuwa*, meaning "grizzly bear fort," and the name of a Native village on Admiralty Island that was famed for its homegrown whiskey. On English tongues, *khutsnuwa* became *hootchinoo*, which was eventually shortened to just hootch or hooch.

HOSER

First popularized in the early 1980s on the Canadian sketch comedy show, SCTV, by Rick Moranis and Dave Thomas, who gleefully embraced the Canadian stereotype, the term hoser describes a particular sort of Canadian. Hosers are clumsy and oafish, presumably because they are constantly drinking beer, and noticeably Canadian, because they wear tuques. As a verb, to hose first entered common Canadian English usage during the 1960s. To hose a hockey team was to soundly beat them; to hose an individual was to interfere with his or her plans. Although often used in a derogatory manner, hoser can be a term of endearment as well.

HOUND POUNDER

As in most Canadian cities, hockey is almost a religion in Sault Ste. Marie, where the Greyhounds of the Ontario Hockey League come to play. Among their many fans are the hound pounders, so named because they really, really, really love the Greyhound players.

HYDRO

Though most people know it as electricity or a utility, to many Canadians, it's hydro. An informal shortening of the Hydro-Electric Commission of Ontario, which was formed in 1906, hydro has become shorthand for the actual power or electricity distributed by a corporation. There's BC Hydro, Ontario Hydro and Québec Hydro, to name just a few power corporations whose governments have adopted the name. So instead of an electrical bill, Canadians pay a hydro bill. When caught in a blackout, they'll say, "hydro's out." Those unfamiliar with the term can be for-given for thinking that it's their taps, and not their refrigerators that have stopped running.

ICE-POOL

A spring event, an ice-pool is a sweepstakes in which the winner is the one who most accurately predicts when the ice will move during the spring break-up. In the days of the Klondike Gold Rush, spring break-up meant much-needed supplies from the south could arrive. A pool describes all the money bet on a particular event by a number of individuals.

ICEWORM

According to the South Tuchone people of the southern Yukon, on winter nights and on days when the sun never rises, the iceworm emerges from its habitat to terrorize trespassing humans. Should a human come near one, the creature attaches itself like a leech to any area of exposed flesh, sucking out all a person's body heat and leaving nothing but dead skin behind. The legend of the iceworm was popularized during the Klondike Gold Rush of the 1890s. Elmer "Stroller" White, a writer with the *Whitehorse Star*, wrote an imaginary tale about the giant iceworm.

The creature had a head on either end of its long, slippery body and came out when the temperature dropped below −60° C. Its smaller brethren, resembling earthworms, were said to be the main component of the iceworm cocktail, a practical joke played on new prospectors by grizzled veterans and immortalized by Robert Service in his poem *The Ballad of the Ice-Worm Cocktail*. There actually is a creature called the ice worm that lives its entire life within glacial ice, in small water pockets near the surface. Ranging from a few millimetres to centimetres in size, the tiny iceworm is a close relative of the earthworm and cannot tolerate temperatures of more than 4° C.

I

IMAX

In 1970, Canadians Graeme Ferguson, Robert Kerr and Roman Kroitor (with the help of friend William Shaw) premiered the film *Tiger Child* at the Fuji Pavilion of the 1970 World's Exposition in Japan. Audiences were stunned to see images splashed across an eight-storey screen so large that it felt as if they had been immersed in the very images themselves. The film had been presented in the newly invented IMAX format. Ferguson, Kerr and Koitor had established themselves with their films *Polar Life* and *Labyrinth*, which debuted at Expo '67 in Montréal. They were multiscreen spectacles that floored audiences and left them wanting more. The problem was that to show these films, multiple cumbersome projectors had to be used. When they were approached by the Japanese to develop a film for their Expo, Kroitor turned to friends Ferguson and Kerr, and with Shaw's engineering assistance, they invented the IMAX projector. An entirely new genre of film was born. While IMAX has become a popular format today to screen blockbusters such as *The Matrix* and the *Harry Potter* films, Ferguson, Kerr and Koitor developed their device to reduce the number of slide and film projectors required to exhibit audio-visual and multimedia presentations.

I

INCONNU

When Alexander Mackenzie was exploring the Northwest Territories, his team of voyageurs encountered a fish the likes of which they had never seen before. They called it simply the *poisson inconnu*, the unknown fish. Today it is known as the largest member of the whitefish family. Although its Latin name is *Stenodus leucichthys*, which means narrow-toothed whitefish, it is still called inconnu. From inconnu comes the corruption *conny* or *connie*, by which the inconnu is also known. The Inuit call the fish *shees*, from which yet another name is drawn: sheefish. Not a bad assortment of names for a fish that was once unknown. The inconnu is found throughout the Northwest Territories and the Yukon. It is a long fish with a wide mouth of small, densely packed teeth. Before 1945, the fish was not caught commercially, although it is now popular in the United States, where its high oil content makes it perfect for the smoked fish industry. It is caught principally in Great Slave Lake.

INUKSUK

In the barren landscapes of the North, eerie and stoic figures rise up from the land, stony, lumbering sentinels that look as old as time. These are the Inuksuit of the Canadian Arctic. Meaning "to act in the capacity of a human being," an Inuksuk is a large figure made of rocks that resembles a human with outstretched arms. Occupying a place in Inuit folklore, these Inuksuit also served a very practical and very basic need. In a landscape of few natural landmarks, the Inuksuit serve as navigational markers, coordination points, message centres and indicators of good hunting and fishing grounds. Inuit hunters often hide behind an Inuksuk to better ambush a herd of caribou.

JOE LOUIS CAKES

To those unfamiliar with these best-selling cakes made in Québec, one might ask why a French Canadian dessert was named after American boxer Joe Louis. It wasn't. In 1923, Arcade Vachon and his wife Rose-Anna moved to Saint-Marie-de-Beauce in Québec to start their own bakery. Initially, they sold just breads, but in 1928, the couple began experimenting with cakes as well. Among these was the Gateau Jos. Louis, named after their two sons, Joseph and Louis. It was anglicized into Joe Louis cakes, confusing generations of Canadians. Joe Louis cakes consist of a layer of vanilla sandwiched between two layers of chocolate cake and then covered with yet more chocolate; the number of recipes available for these snacks testifies to the Joe Louis cakes' continuing popularity.

KAYAK

From the Inuit word for "man's boat," a kayak was originally used by the indigenous peoples of the North and Greenland to hunt on the Arctic Ocean. Made from a light wooden frame and rendered waterproof with a tightly stretched membrane of sealskin, the kayak is a small, one-man canoe steered and propelled with a double-bladed paddle. The paddler sits amidships, feet forward, and is protected from the water by a sprayskirt. Modern versions are used mainly for recreation and come in a host of materials such as plastic, fibreglass and Kevlar.

KEENER

Usually found sitting in the front row of a classroom and fond of asking questions of great irrelevance, keeners have been reviled in Canadian university classrooms for decades. They are known elsewhere as suck-ups, boot-licks and kiss-asses. Overly enthusiastic, eager and intense, keeners make a habit of trying to impress people in authority to further their own ambitions and thereby earn the ire of those around them. While they may be called keeners (after the adjective meaning "intellectually alert"), the term is used ironically and may have, in fact, been derived from another meaning of the word keen. From the Middle English *kene*, keen can also mean pungent and offensive to the nose, which keeners most certainly are. A popular game in university classrooms is Keener Bingo. In Ireland, a keener is a professional funeral mourner.

KEROSENE

Distilled from petroleum in a method invented by Canadian doctor Abraham Gesner, kerosene is a thin, colourless fuel that was once widely used in cooking stoves and hand-held lamps. Gesner first exhibited his discovery in Prince Edward Island in 1846, although he didn't get around to naming it until 1854. He combined the Greek word for wax, *keros*, with the common chemical ending *ene*, to get kerosene. It makes sense, really, because the fuel was used in lamps, replacing the finicky wax candles popular at the time. Today, a variant of high-grade kerosene is used as fuel for jet engines.

KLONDIKE

On July 14, 1897, the steamship *Excelsior* sailed into San Francisco bearing a precious cargo of more than $500,000 in gold that had been panned in the Klondike region of Canada's Yukon Territory. With a severe recession crippling both the United States and Canada, the press fell upon the story like wolves, writing sensational articles about the vast stores of gold just waiting to be panned in the Klondike. The gold rush was on. Prior to 1896, the Yukon was a frontier land, sparsely populated by aborginals, fur traders, prospectors and a few members of the North-West Mounted Police. The territory had a total population of just under 5000 people. The Klondike Gold Rush pushed that number to over 30,000 in just two short years. Dawson City was transformed from a sleepy fishing village into the most cosmopolitan city west of Winnipeg, with stores offering French champagnes, oysters and the latest fashions from Paris. Fortunes were made. In 1897, $2.5 million dollars worth of gold was extracted. A year later, it was $10 million. But as quickly as the rush had begun, it ended. With the discovery of gold at Nome, Alaska in 1899, prospectors fled the Yukon to test their fortunes there. Still, in 1900, over $22 million in gold was extracted from the Yukon. The Klondike itself is a tributary of the Yukon River and is an anglicized version of the Gwich'in word, *tron-duik*, meaning "hammer river."

KOKANEE AND SOCKEYE SALMON

Although kokanee for many people will be nothing but a beer pitched by a man dressed in a Sasquatch costume, it is originally a Kutenai word that translated means "red fish." The Kutenai lived in the Kootenay region of southeastern

British Columbia and southwestern Alberta and often fished the kokanee salmon. Along the Pacific coast, the Salish also had a word for red fish, "suk-kegh," which has been turned into sockeye, of the famous sockeye salmon. Although the fish are not usually red, when the sockeye salmon turns upstream to spawn, its back takes on a brilliant red hue that contrasts sharply with its green head. The sockeye and the kokanee are actually the same fish, although the kokanee may be slightly smaller. The only difference between the two fish is that the kokanee is a land-locked, freshwater sockeye salmon. And seeing as it is a sockeye, the kokanee also turns a bright red colour when spawning, which explains how one fish could have two names.

LABRADOR TEA

Labrador tea is the name of both a small aromatic shrub (*Ledum groenlandicum*) common throughout northeastern North America and the hot beverage made from its narrow, leathery leaves. The shrub is a plant of many uses. For centuries, it was used by North American Indians, such as the Cree, to treat skin ailments and, considering its high content of vitamin C, to prevent scurvy. When Hudson Bay's Company traders began exploring the continent, they too realized its usefulness, finding it particularly effective in treating arthritis, dizziness, stomach troubles, heartburn, colds and tuberculosis. Little surprise then, that Labrador tea is also known as Hudson Bay tea. It thrives in cold bogs and mountain woods and is grazed upon by both caribou and moose. But as effective as the plant can be in treating ailments, use it in small doses. Excessive consumption of Labrador tea can cause blistering headaches and even intoxication, and may be why Laplanders place the bush's leaves in their grain to keep mice away. Placed in clothing, the leaves deter moths. In Russia, the leaves are used in the leather tanning process. Newfoundland and Labrador's coat of arms features a small field of Labrador tea.

LABRADORITE

Named after the Labrador Peninsula where it was first discovered by missionaries in 1770, labradorite is the provincial mineral of Newfoundland. A feldspar, it's a stone composed of silica, alumina, iron, lime, soda and potash, and is deceptively plain. Viewed from one angle, it may appear grey-green. From another, the stone's iridescence, so strong and remarkable that it has become known as labradorescence, reveals itself in a dazzling display of blues, and in rarer cases, yellows, reds and golds. Though used primarily today in jewellery, it was for a time ground and used as an additive in washing powder and a polishing agent in toothpaste. Labradorite has a long and sometimes mystical history. Native American Indians who encountered the stone called it firestone and powdered it for use in potions and magic. Modern-day mystics still ascribe magical qualities to the stone, believing that it can unleash the power of the imagination, amplify a person's strengths, aid in sleep and foster empathy. In Inuit folklore, the Northern Lights were imprisoned within labradorite. An Inuit warrior found them, and with a stab of a mighty spear, freed most of them. The rest remain trapped in labradorite, destined to forever shimmer and dazzle.

LACROSSE

The oldest organized sport in North America, lacrosse was first played by aboriginal peoples, including the Iroquois and Cherokee. For them, it was far more than just a sport. Called baggataway or teewaraathon, it was a sacred ritual and was viewed as the Creator's Game. Hundreds or even thousands of people would spend days at the game, running across fields that spanned as much as 24 km to lob a clay or stone ball at a tree marker. People viewed the game as a training ground for war; the Cherokee called it "the little brother of war." Early French explorers who witnessed these events saw something familiar. The sticks, they felt, resembled a bishop's crozier, which they called *la crosse*. The game itself may have resembled a field hockey game called *jeu de la crosse* that the French often played. Modern lacrosse embodies elements of basketball, soccer and hockey, and the rules for the modern game were laid down in the late 19th century by Dr. William George Peers, a Montréal-based dentist.

LATEER

An anglicized version of the French Canadian word *la tire*, lateer is what you get when you pour hot maple syrup into the snow: brittle shards of sugary goodness popular throughout Québec with all ages (though they call it *tire sur la neige*). *La tire* is French Canadian for toffee, and it was derived from the French verb, *tirer*, to pull, a literal description of how toffee is made.

LCBO

In 1927, after an 11-year experiment, the Ontario Temperance Act was repealed. Prohibition was over. With the province wet again, the government, still concerned about people's consumption of alcohol, created the Liquor Control Board of Ontario—the LCBO. Established by the Liquor Control Act, the LCBO would control the sale, transportation and delivery of alcoholic beverages in Ontario and would regulate the availability and consumption of alcohol. In 1927, the first LCBO stores opened in Toronto, and soon there were 80 across the province. Sales were over $12.3 million. Today, the LCBO has over 600 stores, employs about 5000 people and generates sales of $2 billion. It is one of the largest single purchasers of alcohol in the world. In 1997, consumers were allowed to buy alcohol on Sundays. In Ontario, LCBO has become synonymous for the liquor store, and people can often be heard in Toronto's downtown core saying, "I can't believe this LCBO closes at 6 on a Saturday." In recent years, the Ontario government has flirted with the idea of privatizing the sale of liquor, meaning that the LCBO may soon be nothing but a memory.

LOBSTICK

The northern Cree used a lobstick as a living landmark: a tribute or a monument to a friend, perhaps, or as a personal talisman or a geographic marker in a land that could swallow up even the hardiest and knowledgeable of explorers. The lobstick itself was a conspicuous thing, a spruce or pine tree that had been denuded of all its branches save for the topmost and two bottom ones. The earliest voyageurs used lobsticks as trailmarkers over 200 years ago. The great explorer Alexander Mackenzie coined the name for these strange and eerie monuments in his 1789 book, *Voyage from Montréal*.

LOONIE

In May 1987, the Canadian government, in an attempt to cut costs, introduced an 11-sided, gold-coloured coin to replace the one-dollar bill. The move wasn't a popular one and in jest, Canadians took to calling the coin "Mulroney's Loonie," after then Prime Minister Brian Mulroney. Not only did the term rhyme, but loonie perfectly described the new coin. Made of aureate bronze plated onto pure nickel, the loonie depicts on its reverse side a loon drifting lazily through a lake. On the obverse is a portrait of Queen Elizabeth II. The loon was designed by famed wildlife artist Robert-Ralph Carmichael, but it was not the original intended design. The plan was to have a voyageur, but he got lost during his portage to the Royal Canadian Mint in Winnipeg. No matter. The loon is Canada's national bird and while it didn't gain popularity until 1989 when the Royal Canadian Bank stopped producing one-dollar bills, the coin quickly became common, weighing down the pockets and purses of Canadians everywhere. The name loonie stuck.

LOTUS LAND

It's not clear when Canadians began referring to British Columbia as Lotus Land, but it probably has something to do with the province's laid-back, relaxed and easy-going attitude. With a temperate climate, beautiful beaches and proximity to both the ocean and the Rockies, British Columbians are able to enjoy their leisure and care little if stressed easterners cluck their tongues and turn their noses up. Lotus Land as a term for a land of dreamy and languid contentment is drawn from Homer's *The Odyssey*, in which Odysseus journeyed to the land of the Lotus-Eaters, where people lived in a blissful, drugged and indolent state. While British Columbians use the term with pride, the term Lotus Land does have pejorative overtones, associated as it is with laziness and lives devoted to little else besides pleasure and luxury.

MAL DE RAQUETTE

Mal de raquette, or snowshoe sickness, was the bane of many of Canada's earliest explorers. Aboriginals used snowshoes with the greatest of ease, but the coureurs de bois, often found that the muscles of their legs and feet were ill-prepared for the rigours of tramping across the snow on the raquette, or snowshoe. Novice users of snowshoes are advised today to tread lightly and avoid the mal de raquette.

MALPEQUE OYSTERS

Although just a tiny province, Prince Edward Island looms large in the culinary world because in Malpeque Bay, PEI, Malpeque oysters are grown. Prized for their buttery texture and sharp-sweet, briny flavour, Malpeques can fetch as much as $3 per single oyster at some restaurants in New York, arguably the culinary capital of North America. The first Prince Edward Island product to be widely exported, Malpeques are still harvested by fishermen using traditional hand-held rakes. When the winter ice begins to break up, fishermen head out in 16-foot long dories to rake the mud to expose the oysters that are just beginning to feed again after a long winter's hibernation. Malpeque Bay is an Acadian French translation of the Mi'kmaq word, *Mak Paak*, meaning "large bay."

MAPLE SYRUP AND ITS TERMS

As the world's leading producer of maple syrup, Québec has developed a language all its own to describe the various aspects of the maple syrup industry. It produces close to 90 percent of Canada's maple syrup and sells its product all around the globe. A lot of maple syrup terms revolve around the word sugar, which is the main component of maple syrup and why consumers love the stuff so much. Native peoples, especially those living in the St. Lawrence and Great Lakes regions, have been drawing syrup from maple trees for centuries. They used an innovative and practical method of boiling down the sap. The Algonquin called the sap *sinzibuckwud*, meaning "drawn from wood." Legend has it that the syrup was discovered by the Iroquois, who often cooked their meat in maple sap. At some point, they began collecting sap in hollowed-out logs they called *mococks*. Stones were then heated and tossed into the logs, boiling the water off. French explorers sampled the product and quickly fell in love with it. In 1690, a Frenchman is believed to have been the first European to make maple syrup, and with so many stands of maple native throughout the

Maritimes, southern Ontario and Québec (and as the only source of sugar available to settlers), the industry flourished. *Maple sugaring,* the harvesting and processing of maple syrup, had become a community event by the 18th century. The sap was collected during three runs: *the robin run, the frog run* and *the bud run.* The *sugarshack* became the building where water from the sap, collected in stands of maple trees called a *sugarbush,* was boiled off under the watchful eye of the *sugarmaster.* The maple leaf has adorned our national flag since it was first unveiled on February 15, 1965, and on April 25, 1996, it became Canada's national arboreal emblem.

MARQUIS WHEAT
In the mid- to late 19th century, settlers were beginning to populate the vast prairies of the Canadian West, lured there by the cheap land and the convenience and ease of the railway. But the prairie weather was harsh, and farming proved difficult in the short growing season. The Red Fife wheat that was grown, while hardy, was easily damaged by frost. William Saunders, working at Ottawa's Central Experiment Farm, decided to rectify the problem. Along with his son Charles, Saunders spent almost 10 years cross-breeding countless wheat varieties in the hopes of creating a durable wheat that matured quickly. In 1909, the Saunders unveiled the fruit of their labours: Marquis wheat, a cross between Red Fife and Hard Red Calcutta. Introduced to the West

in 1910, it proved hardy, had high yields and matured three to ten days faster than the Red Fife, and could therefore be harvested before the onset of frost. Marquis wheat opened the prairies, doubling the amount of land that could be farmed. By 1920, 90 percent of Canadian wheat being grown was of the Marquis variety. William Saunders and his son were single-handedly responsible for turning the Canadian West into the breadbasket of the world. When Sir Charles Saunders died in 1937, the *London Daily Express* wrote in his obituary that "he added more wealth to his country than any other man. Marconi gave power. Saunders gave abundance. Great lives, these."

MARSH PEGS

He may not have ever fulfilled his dream of playing in the National Hockey League, but Fred Marsh can claim something that not even the greatest hockey players such as Wayne Gretzky or Bobby Orr can. Since 1991, a part of Fred Marsh has been at every NHL game, every playoff game and every Stanley Cup final game. He's even been to the Olympics twice and to the World Cup. How has he accomplished this feat? Marsh's story begins in British Columbia, where he worked in arenas for four decades. In 1984, the community of Kitimat was concerned about the injuries hockey players were sustaining after crashing into the metal posts of the goalie's net. Anchored by rigid metal rods, the nets had little give. Legs were broken and careers were aborted. Marsh set about creating Marsh Pegs, which would allow the net to move but not enough to dislodge it during play. If a player crashes into it, the net comes loose, thereby decreasing the chances of injury. In 1991, the National Hockey League began using Marsh Pegs, too, and at long last, at the age of 56, Fred Marsh had made it to the big show.

MCINTOSH APPLES

If it weren't for a family squabble and an unfortunate love, the world might never have known the pleasures and delights of eating the sweet, red, crisp fruit known as the McIntosh. In 1796, John McIntosh was living in the Mohawk Valley of New York state with his Scottish parents. But, after a family feud over a girl McIntosh had fallen in love with, he headed north to meet his love, whom he planned to marry in secret. But when he arrived, he discovered that she had passed away, the victim of a sudden and unexpected illness. Distraught and heartbroken, McIntosh settled near Prescott, Ontario, in a little farming community named Dundela. While clearing his land in 1811, McIntosh made a serendipitous discovery. Several young apple trees were growing on his land; McIntosh transplanted them to a garden near his home. One tree in particular bore an apple of such sweetness and crispness that family and friends clamoured for more. They even wanted their own trees, but unfortunately, McIntosh and others could not replicate nature's work. Finally in 1835, McIntosh, on the advice of a farmhand, succeeded when he tried the techniques of grafting and budding. From that one tree came millions of others, each bearing apples that became known as McIntosh Reds. Today, there are over three million McIntosh trees throughout North America, and the McIntosh comprises almost half of Canada's annual apple crop.

MEDICARE

On July 1, 1962, the Co-operative Commonwealth Federation government of Saskatchewan finally introduced its Medical Care Act. It was the realization of a dream that had begun when Premier Tommy Douglas, widely acknowledged as the "Father of Medicare," had been first elected in 1944. As early as 1933, the CCF's *Regina Manifesto* stated that "health services should be made at least as freely available as are educational services today...under this system that is namely a private enterprise...costs of proper medical care are prohibitive to the great masses of the people." Ironically, those words are relevant today. The act's passage introduced a new word to Canadians: Medicare, defined as publicly funded and universal health care. It's also a word charged with political and social significance. From its inception, the Medical Care Act was wildly unpopular with Saskatchewan doctors, who staged a 23-day strike in protest. They feared that it would threaten their livelihoods and destroy the patient-doctor relationship. The great experiment turned out to be a great success and, in 1967, Medicare went national with the passage of the Canada Health Act.

MEMORIAL CUP

In March 1919, the Ontario Hockey Association donated a trophy called the OHA Memorial Cup, so named to honour the fallen Canadian soldiers of the First World War. It would be awarded to the top junior hockey team in Canada. From 1919 to 1928, two teams, one from eastern Canada and one from western Canada, met in a two-game, total-goals series to determine the recipient of the Memorial Cup. From 1929 to 1971, the championship was decided in a best-of-three series. In 1972, the commissioners of the Canadian Hockey League decided that the three champions of its three leagues, the Western Hockey League, the Québec Major Junior Hockey League and the Ontario Hockey League, met in a round-robin tournament to determine the cup winner. In 1983, a fourth team, the host team, was added.

MÉTIS

The Métis are Canadian aboriginals of First Nation and European ancestry. The term has been in use since the earliest days of the fur trade to describe the offspring of French and Scottish traders and their Cree, Ojibwa, Saulteaux and Assiniboine wives. The Métis evolved into their own peoples in the historic northwest, with their own customs and language, *Michif*, a mixture of French and Cree that employed French nouns and noun phrases within the Cree verb system. Their culture reflects the diversity of their origins, incorporating Scottish, French, Ojibway and Cree traditions. The annexation of their land by Canada in 1869 crippled their economy, and for years afterwards, they became known as Canada's forgotten people. It wasn't until 1982 that they were officially recognized as an aboriginal people in the Canadian Constitution. Estimates place today's Métis population at anywhere between 300,000 and 800,000 people, most of whom live in western Canada. The word Métis is drawn from the French word for mixed, which itself is derived from the Latin word *miscellus*. Famous Métis heroes include Louis Riel and Gabriel Dumont.

MICKEY or MICKY

Usually found shoved down pants, a mickey, or micky, refers to a 384 ml bottle of liquor, usually whiskey, and often shaped to fit, conveniently, in a pocket. The term gained popularity in the middle of the 19th century, when the bottles became popular with those looking to hide their prodigious drinking. Although it seems only Canadians use the term in this way, the mickey's origins are Irish and American. In the late 19th century, New York City's Irish immigrant population was exploding, and with bigotry hounding their every step, many Irishmen turned to the bars for comfort. Mickey Finn became slang for a rowdy and drunk Irishman. It was first applied to liquor itself in the early 20th century. According to legend, a Chicago bar named Mickey Finn gained great notoriety for its drink specials. Spiked, the drinks contained chloral hydrate, rendering unconscious anyone who drank them. Once knocked out, unsuspecting patrons were taken to a back room, robbed and then dumped in an alley. Other bars adopted this sort of Mickey Finn, but instead of chloral hydrate, they used laxatives, dropping them only into the drinks of the most unruly and belligerent customers. It was the easiest way of getting the overly inebriated to leave in a hurry.

MINTY
Just so there's no confusion, when a person from Winnipeg calls something minty, he isn't saying that it smells like peppermint or that it's fragrant. Minty is a catch-all expression in Winnipeg. It means cool or fantastic or, in some cases, it just means something is mint, as in mint condition. The origins of the term are unknown, though perhaps it relates to the Royal Canadian Mint being headquartered there.

MOLSON MUSCLE
Although its origins are obscure, Molson muscle is a distinctly Canadian term used to describe the pot

belly, the beer belly or the spare tire, essentially, an enlarged gut resulting from the consumption of too many Molson Canadians. The alliterative term is much more flattering—it almost sounds like something you could and should be proud of.

MUKLUK

Originally made from the skins of the bearded seal or the reindeer, the mukluk was a knee-high boot, soft, warm and waterproof. Within the etymology of the word lies the mukluk's origin; mukluk is derived from the Yupik word *maklak*, meaning "bearded seal." Yupik was a language of the Inuit of the western Arctic. The word has entered Canadian English and is now applied to any slipper with a soft sole resembling the mukluk. Today mukluks are made from all sorts of synthetic materials.

MUSKELLUNGE

Prized by anglers for its ferocity and tenacity, the muskellunge (or musky, as it's also known) is a powerful predator closely related to the northern pike. It is the largest of Canada's freshwater game fish, and though most caught today weigh just between 2.3 and 16.3 kilograms, some have been known to exceed 45 kilograms. Found through-out the St. Lawrence River, the Great Lakes and some inland waters in Ontario and Québec, the muskellunge derives its name from the Ojibwa word, *maskingonge*, meaning "ugly fish" and *lunge*, or "lake trout." Some linguists have also offered the idea that muskellunge may be a corruption of the French *maggue allongee,* or "long face," which is what early French explorers may have called this fighting fish.

MUSKOX

To the northern Indians, it is known as *omingmak*—the animal with skin like a beard. Given its woolly appearance and long skirt of fur that hangs to the ground, it's easy to see why it was given such a name. But early Canadian fur traders, who prized the muskox for its fur, called it something else entirely. They named the creature the muskox, because of its resemblance to the ox and because of the musky smell of its urine, especially during mating season. One of Canada's oldest mammals, the muskox is uniquely adapted to life in the arctic tundra. Its coat is made of two layers, one hairy and one woolly. Its wool, known as *qiviut* to the Inuit, is stronger than sheep's wool, and finer and eight times warmer than cashmere. Not surprisingly, the muskox was prized for its coat and its meat. Its horns were used for Inuit tools and crafts. Often seen standing in outward facing circles to harness their warmth and to protect their young, muskoxen can survive temperatures of –40° C, high winds and blowing snow. Human hunters exploited the muskoxen's defensive circles, using dogs to act as arctic wolves, the muskox's only natural predator, and then using spears and arrows to slay the massed animals. In

1917, the Canadian government brought the muskox under its protection, and the animal now roams in great numbers across the Banks and Victoria Islands of Canada's North.

NANAIMO BAR

The origins of the Nanaimo bar are unclear. According to one account, the Nanaimo bar was first created about 35 years ago when a Nanaimo housewife decided to enter a magazine cooking contest. She dubbed her entry—a sweet chocolate and buttercream concoction—Nanaimo bars. The treat won raves and a prize, forever linking that Vancouver Island community with the dessert. It proved so popular that it wasn't long before the recipe was made available as a handout, printed onto tea towels and souvenir aprons for Canadians from all over the country eager to duplicate the confection in their own kitchens. However, northeastern Americans claim that the Nanaimo bar has its roots in New York, where it has been known for years as a New York Slice. Still others claim that the Nanaimo bar became popular during that community's mining heydays in the 19th century. Many of the miners who flocked to Nanaimo to plumb its coal-rich depths had come from the United Kingdom. Far removed from their homes and families, they often asked their

N

distant relatives to send them care packages. Nestled among their boxes of tea and biscuits were chocolate squares. These proved popular not just with the miners, but with the locals too, and eventually, they became known as Nanaimo bars. Regardless of its origins, the Nanaimo bar is firmly entrenched as a much-beloved item on the Canadian menu. At its most basic, it consists of a base of chocolate and coconut, a buttercream centre and a chocolate glaze. There are countless variations, with some recipes incorporating whole nuts, peanut butter and other items, all deliciously addictive.

OKA CHEESE

Oka was first made in 1893 in the little Québec village of Oka. It was first produced by French Trappist monks and was a variation of a Port Salut recipe that had come from Brittany. Monks still oversee the cheese's production, ensuring that the semi-soft cheese with the pungent aroma and creamy taste will continue to reach standards of excellence.

OOLICHAN

To the aboriginals of Canada's northern coasts, the arrival of the oolichan often signalled the end of yet another long, harsh winter. Known as the "salvation fish," the oolichan was the first fish to arrive in the rivers of spring, a welcome sight for the early people whose food stores had almost been depleted. A small, silvery fish, the oolichan (*Thaleichthys pacificus*) is a member of the smelt family, usually growing between 15 and 20 cm long and weighing between 40 and 60 gr. The flesh was sometimes eaten, but the fish was and is prized more for its oil. Northern First Nations all have different methods of obtaining oolichan grease, with each producing slightly different flavours. Typically the oolichan are allowed to ripen under evergreen branches for two weeks and then are cooked in fresh water. The oil is then skimmed from the top to be used, like butter, on salmon, halibut or berries. The grease trails of British Columbia derive their name from the oolichan grease trade.

0

PABLUM

In 1931, after two years of research at the Hospital for Sick Children in Toronto, three doctors, Frederick Tisdall, Theodore Drake and Alan Brown, unveiled the fruit of their labours. It was called Pablum, derived from the Latin *pabulum*, which means food or animal feed. The doctors' mixture of wheat, oats, corn, bone meal, wheat germ, dried brewer's yeast and alfalfa gave to the world its very first thoroughly cooked, dried and nutritious cereal for infants. Although it tasted terribly bland, the concoction was packed full of five vitamins: A, B_1, B_2, D and E. It was the vitamin D that was most important; the doctors were intent on preventing rickets, a disease that develops in early childhood owing to a lack of that particular vitamin. Free of eggs, dairy and nuts, it was also unlikely to cause allergic reactions. Given its simple, bland flavour and its place as a staple of any infant's diet, the term pablum has also become slang for oversimplified ideas.

PAINT ROLLER

In the 1930s, Norman Breakey of Toronto decided to change the world of painting and design, and to get rich doing it, too. In 1940, he unveiled his idea: the paint roller. People loved the t-shaped device for its simplicity and the way in which it chopped hours off of the arduous task of painting with a brush. Unfortunately, its very simplicity proved to be Breakey's undoing. Imitations of his device popped up everywhere, and though Breakey had patented his invention, he couldn't afford to legally defend it, so the riches that he had envisioned never did materialize. Breakey is credited with revolutionizing the painting and design industry and for ushering in a whole new do-it-yourself movement, but it was of little comfort to him.

PEAMEAL BACON

To most Americans, Canadian bacon is what we call back bacon, a smoked pork product that tastes and looks a lot like ham. But many Canadians (at least those in Ontario), will tell you that real Canadian bacon is actually peameal bacon. Peameal bacon consists of a boneless pork loin, cured in pickle brine, and then rolled in ground yellow peas. The ground yellow peas helped cure the pork and added vastly to its shelf life. The yellow peas are no longer used (they've been replaced by cornmeal), but the name has stuck. How did Canadian bacon become Canadian bacon? According to Ken Haviland, who was born in Ontario but who now lives in Wisconsin, a pork shortage in England at the end of the 19th century led to the importing of side bacon from Canada. The English smoked the meat, and Americans who sampled the product were told that it had come from Canada. Peameal bacon was left for Canadians to savour.

PEMMICAN

From the Abnaki word *pemikan* and the Cree word *pimikan* (meaning "prepared fat"), pemmican was the food upon which Canada was built. Nutritious, hearty and durable, pemmican was prized by North American Indians and fur traders. Fatty buffalo meat provided both iron and energy, while the berries proved especially useful at warding off scurvy. Pemmican was the major food staple of Alexander Mackenzie when he became the first European to cross the North American continent in 1793. To make pemmican, dried strips of meat from animals such as bison, moose, elk or deer were ground and pounded between stones. To the meat, ground berries were added along with the melted fat, suet and bone marrow grease. The mixture was then stored in bags made of bison skin, called *parfleches*, which were sealed with melted tallow. As the bison skins dried, they shrank, compressing the meat and creating an airtight container that preserved the pemmican for years. There are records of traders consuming pemmican that had kept for four years. They are said to have recorded no noticeable difference in taste or texture.

PENGUIN

The original penguin was not the breed with which we are familiar today. The term penguin was first used to describe a large, flightless, short-necked diving seabird known as the great auk (*Pinguinus impennis*), which could be found in great abundance on Newfoundland's Funk Island, far removed from Antarctica and the Southern Hemisphere. In the 16th century, the birds were so numerous that they formed a black mass large and distinct enough that early explorers, including Jacques Cartier, used it as a navigational marker. Funk Island became known as the Island of Penguins. The bird itself was valued as a food source, rich in proteins and nutritious fats and oils. Its distinctive feathers were prized for clothing. The word penguin has many origins; some believe that it is a derivation of pen-winged or pinioned. Still others say that it has Welsh roots, from the phrase *pen gwyn*, meaning "white head." The penguin did, after all, have distinctive white patches in front of its eyes. European explorers in the Southern Hemisphere, glimpsing a bird that looked very much like the penguin they had seen in the north, transferred the name to the flightless birds we know today as penguins. The name might have survived, but the bird did not. By 1844, the great auk had been hunted into extinction.

PÉQUISTE

Formed in 1968, the Parti Québecois is a provincial political party dedicated to obtaining independence for Québec. In 1976, under the leadership of René Lévesque, the Parti Québecois gained control of the provincial assembly and quickly passed Bill 101, making French the province's only official language and banned the use of English on signs. However, in 1980, a provincial referendum rejected plans to open talks with the federal government to negotiate Québec independence. When Lévesque left the party in 1985, the party struggled, returning to power only in 1994. A year later, the party stumbled again when plans for independence were narrowly rejected in a hotly contested referendum. In the 2003 election, the Parti Québecois, led by Bernard Landry, lost to Jean Charest's Liberal Party. The party's tenacious supporters and members are known as péquistes, a derivation of the French pronunciation of the party's initials.

PINGO

From the Inuit word *pingu*, which means "ice-lens," a pingo is an ice-cored hill, typically conical in shape. Water and ice that has accumulated underground is pushed upward, breaking through the surface. Exposed, it begins to collect peat and soil, thus creating the pingo. A pingo is a naturally occurring topographical formation found commonly in areas of permafrost, notably the Canadian Arctic. In the Mackenzie Delta region there are at least 1450 pingos.

PLOYES

A ploye is the Acadian version of a pancake, but unlike the pancake, a ploye uses no milk or eggs in its preparation. It's a versatile item that is often substituted for bread. In some Maritime provinces and Québec, the ploye is eaten at breakfast with cretons, at lunch with some butter and after dinner with berries and whipping cream. Little wonder that it was once a staple of the loggers' diet and continues to be a staple today. Made of buckwheat flour, which was a common, cheap and hardy crop, ployes are cooked on one side only, on a sizzling hot skillet known as a *poëlonne*. The etymology of ploye is not completely clear; some linguists theorize that the word came from the French verb *plier*, "to bend or to fold," which many people do with their ployes. Others speculate that it may have come from the sound of the ploye batter being mixed—ploye, ploye, ploye. Regardless, it is a popular dish throughout eastern Canada, the northeastern United States and Louisiana.

POGEY

When the Great Depression swept through Canada in the 1930s, millions of people found themselves without a job and without an income. The federal government began offering financial assistance for the most distressed of its citizens. Canadians began referring to the money meted out as pogey. Originally used to describe a workhouse, a poorhouse or a prison near the end of the 19th century, pogey has entered Canadian English vernacular. Like the dole in the United Kingdom, pogey is a mildly insulting term for what were once known as unemployment benefits, but which, in this time of overwhelming political correctness, is now known as EI or Employment Insurance.

POT-EN-POT

When the Acadians were expelled from their homes in the Maritimes in 1755, many of them settled in the Magdelan Islands, a crescent-shaped group of islands in the Gulf of St. Lawrence. They brought with them their culture and their foods and even today, centuries later, their influence can be felt in all aspects of life on the islands. One regional specialty is the pot-en-pot, a dish consisting of seafood and potatoes baked in a flaky crust. Its name was derived from the preparation of the dish—two pots were used, the contents of one poured into the other. In Québec, the pot-en-pot is also a meat dish, usually made with chicken and hare, although beef, pork, duck and goose are also used.

POTLATCH

From Chinook Jargon comes the word potlatch, meaning "to give." It is used to describe a ceremonial feast among aboriginal peoples of the northwest Pacific coast given to celebrate the occasion of a marriage or an accession. Historically, the host of a potlatch distributed gifts according to a guest's rank and status, with the implicit under-standing that the host would be treated in kind. Gifts ranged from foods, slaves and copper plates to things less material, such as names, songs or dances. It became popular at potlatches for hosts, desperate to maintain some semblance of nobil-ity and status within a society that could not pos-sibly compete with the industrialized world, to destroy property in an extravagant display, as if to say, "I'll just get another." The Government of Canada banned potlatches in 1884 but even-tually lifted the ban in 1951.

POUTINE

Like many inventions, poutine was conceived through an act of serendipity. In 1957, to satisfy a customer's craving for both French fries and cheese curds, Québec restaurateur Fernand Lachance put both in the same bag. Lachance called the sticky, oozing mess that he had created poutine, which was an early French Canadian derivation of the English word *pudding*, used originally to describe a mish-mash of cookies, custard and fruit. A phenomenon was born. Eventually, gravy was added to the combination of fries and curds, rendering it even more irre-sistible. Poutine has become a food staple beyond Québec. Countries such as Italy have even cooked up their own versions, serving the snack

P

with a meat sauce instead of gravy. Even fast food chains such as McDonald's and Burger King have offered their own versions of the snack.

POVERTY PACK

Perhaps this term, describing a six-pack of beer, originated during the Great Depression. With limited funds and little else to do but drink and escape their numbing realities, the unemployed could only afford the six-pack. Whatever its origins, the poverty pack can be used to describe any six-pack of beer.

PRAIRIE

Prairie is used to refer to the great expanse of mostly flat, rolling and usually treeless grassland covering much of western Canada east of the Rockies and west of the Ontario border. The word prairie comes to Canadian English from the Old French word *praierie*, itself derived from the Latin *pratu*, meaning "meadow," used by French Canadian trappers exploring the continent for pelts.

PUCK

A frozen disc, 7.6 cm in diameter, and made of vulcanized rubber, the puck is the hotly contested object lying at the heart of hockey. It was first used during a hockey game in 1860, at Kingston Harbor, Ontario, replacing the India-rubber ball. How the rubber disc got its name is a mystery. Most believe that it is a derivation of the British dialectical verb, to puck (poke), meaning "to hit or to strike" as in "he pucked the ball." Puck is no longer a verb but a noun; now, people shout "shoot the puck" or "stop the puck!"

QUÉBECOIS

When Champlain built a blockhouse on Cape Diamond in 1608 overlooking the St. Lawrence River, it was hard not to notice that the river narrowed at the point. The Mi'kmaqs called the area *Gepeeg*, or "where the river narrows." From that word, came Québec, and subsequently, Québecois. Although Québecois, at its simplest, refers to a resident of Québec, especially one who speaks French, it is a word fraught with meaning and significance. For many Anglophones, Québecois symbolizes those agitating for political and social independence in Québec, an association no doubt born out of the 1976 election in which the Parti Québecois ran and won on a platform of sovereignty.

RED ROSE TEA

Who can forget the television ads for Red Rose tea, in which a stuffy British gentleman sniffs, "Only in Canada, you say? Pity?" Red Rose, the tea available only in Canada, has its beginnings with Theodore Estabrooks. In 1894, Estabrooks, who worked as an importer and exporter, decided to specialize in tea. From the start, it looked as if Estabrooks had made a terrible decision. He sold only just $166 dollars worth of his product in his first year. But, in 1899, Estabrooks teamed with a friend, M.R. Miles, to create something new and different. Teas at the time were usually a blend of Chinese and Japanese teas. Estabrooks and Miles looked south, to India and Sri Lanka, and created a blend of tea that they called Red Rose Tea. The blend met with great success and by 1900, Estabrooks' company was selling over 1000 tons of tea a year. Headquartered in St. John, New Brunswick, Red Rose found fans throughout that province and Nova Scotia, and eventually the rest of the country.

R

REEVE

Common in Ontario and some parts of western Canada, a reeve is the elected head of a township council or a rural municipal council. Derived from Middle and Old English, a reeve, in Anglo-Saxon times, was a high administrative officer appointed by a king. Later, the term also came to apply to manor officers who overlooked feudal discharges.

REGALE

As a noun, regale can mean a great feast, or a great delicacy, or some sort of refreshment. Whatever its definition, it's clear that a regale appeals to both the appetite and desire. It's no wonder then, that the fur-traders and trappers of the Hudson's Bay Company used the French word to describe the special ration of rum they received on festive occasions and after a long and tortuous journey. The word survives today in Canadian English, but has come to encompass any handout or favour given at a party.

ROUGHRIDER

Originally a British term used to describe a non-commissioned officer of the British Cavalry and assistant to the riding master, a roughrider became something else during the settlement of the West. Horses were crucial to survival on the open prairies, and men who could break wild steeds for domestic use were rare and therefore prized. Accustomed to the rough and hard riding of a wild horse, these men became known as roughriders. They shouldn't be confused with Canadian Football League teams in Saskatchewan or Ottawa, or with the members of the Rough Riders cavalry regiment that fought under U.S. President Theodore Roosevelt during the Spanish-American War.

SAQ

In 1898, a Canada-wide referendum on Prohibition was held. Given its Catholic heritage (wine was used for communion services) and Gallic love of the drink, most Québec voters response was resoundingly negative. Still, in 1918, the Québec government passed Prohibition legislation. Just a year later, in a province-wide referendum, Québecers voted to exclude beer, wine and cider from the Prohibition law, and Québec became the only jurisdiction in both Canada and the United States not to have total Prohibition. To regulate the sale of wine and spirits, the Québec government passed the Alcoholic Beverages Act in 1921, creating the Commission des Liqueurs du Québec. It opened 64 stories, employed 415 people and, in a testament to the unpopularity of temperance, recorded $15 million in sales. These first stores were nothing but counters set behind a metal grid where only the price list was available for viewing. Patrons could buy only one bottle of spirits a time, and the bottles were wrapped in nondescript paper. In 1941, purchase limits on spirits were abolished, and in 1961, under the newly created Régis des alcohols du Québec, the first partial self-serve stores were opened. In 1971, the Régis des alcohols du Québec was split into two separate entities: the Commission de contrôle des permis d'alcool and the Société des alcools du Québec, which would become more familiarly and fondly known as the SAQ (pronounced sack). Much like the LCBO in Ontario, SAQ in Québec has become slang for the liquor store.

SASHAY

Sashay is an anglicized version of the French word *chasser*, meaning "to chase," and has been in use since the mid-19th century. Brought to Canadian shores by early French explorers, a sashay is a gliding step used in both ballet and square dancing. Informally, it is used, often with derogatory overtones, to describe an effeminate stride.

SCREECH

Screech is short for Newfoundland screech, a particularly potent brand of rum and a traditional drink in the province. Demerara rum from the West Indies was often traded in exchange for Newfoundland salt fish. The rum was a drink with no name and was served in a simple, unlabelled glass bottle. During World War II, the United States established bases throughout Newfoundland. One evening, an American serviceman was out drinking and was tempted to try the shots of liquor that the locals downed in great numbers and with great ease. The American serviceman followed suit, throwing back his drink in one gulp. It didn't agree with him and he let out such a scream that people came running from blocks around to see what the commotion was about. An American sergeant entered the bar, demanding to know what was the reason behind such a "horrible screech." The Newfoundlander who greeted the sergeant at the door simply replied, "The screech? It was the rum." The name stuck, and the government began calling its rum Newfoundland screech. Demerara rum is no longer used; Newfoundland screech is now Jamaica rum, which is far less likely to induce fits of screeching.

SCREECH-IN CEREMONY

For non-native Newfoundlanders who are dying to become Newfoundlanders, there's only one way to go about it: take part in a screech-in ceremony. Performed under the watch of a native Newfoundlander, the screech-in ceremony involves kissing an actual fish (usually a cod, but any other fish will do) on the lips. Then, a shot of screech is lifted high, and just before drinking, the words, "Long may your long jib draw" are uttered. Those successfully completing a screech-in ceremony are forever honorary Newfoundlanders.

SHANTY

A shanty, a roughly and crudely built cabin, may have had its origins in French Canada. Loggers working in the woods often lived in meager, austere conditions, in ramshackle huts they called *chantiers* (which is French for lumberyard). The term had become generalized by, at the latest, the early 19th century. Others hypothesize that the term may have come from Irish immigrants. The Irish Gaelic for old hut is *sean tigh*, and many Irish Canadians worked in the woods of Upper Canada, where the word shanty is believed to have originated.

SHEBANG

Since the mid-19th century, a shebang has been used to describe a hut or shed. It can also be a tavern in the bush, a place for weary trappers and traders to rest and carouse. Its origins are Canadian French from the word *cabane* (meaning "hut") but may also have roots in the Irish Gaelic *shebeen*, which also means hut.

SHIVAREE

A Latin custom, and practised for centuries in France, a shivaree is a custom that was brought to Acadia by the French and then transplanted throughout the continent, notably into Louisiana and Mississippi when the Acadians were expelled. Originally known in French as a *charivari*, shivaree is the French-Canadian form of the word. A shivaree is described as a noisy mock serenade given to newlywed couples. In more superstitious times, it was believed that evil spirits would bring harm to newlyweds. To drive these evil spirits away, guests would bang pans and kettles together, driving the spirits (and presumably anyone within earshot) away.

SIEVE

Heard often in Canada, especially during the hockey season, the word sieve is usually uttered with great frustration and consternation. It's not uncommon to walk through a sports bar and hear, and hear often, "He's such a sieve!" The fans are not referring to the kitchen utensil, but to the goalie. It's not much of a compliment. A sieve, in hockey slang, is a lousy goalie, one prone to letting in too many goals. Sieve, as a word, has its roots in Old and Middle English, from the words *sife* and *sive*. In all likelihood, some kitchen-savvy hockey broadcaster, perhaps Foster Hewitt (who uttered the immortal words, "He shoots, he scores!"), probably gave the word its slang definition.

SIR LAURIER D'ARTHABASKA

Sir Wilfrid Laurier was the first French Canadian prime minister of Canada; elected in 1896, he served until 1911. He lived in Arthabaska, Québec, from 1876 until 1919. The Kingsey Dairy in Québec created a cheese in his honour and named it Sir Laurier d'Arthabaska. A soft, washed-rind cheese with a copper-orange rind and an ivory, creamy interior, it has won numerous awards and is quickly becoming a favourite of many Canadian cheese connoisseurs.

SKOOKUM

A holdover from Chinook Jargon, skookum is perhaps the most common and popular Jargon word still in common use in British Columbia. Originally, skookum meant big, strong and good. It came from the Chehalis language, in which *skukm* denoted power and bravery. Today, skookum is used in a number of ways. If something "looks pretty skookum," then it looks solid and indestructible. If "that's skookum," it means you've done a good job. On its own, "Skookum!" is Chinook Jargon's very own cool, or awesome or excellent. Not surprisingly, a jail along the Pacific coast is sometimes referred to as the skookum box or skookum-house.

SLOB ICE

Slob ice is a term that originated in Newfoundland, but has since spread throughout Canada. Originally it referred to heavy masses of slushy or broken ice, snow and freezing water floating out at sea; slob ice was notoriously difficult to pass through, as it was often a tacky mess. Throughout Canada, it refers to the slush that forms when snow melts upon roadways. The origins of the term are Scandinavian and Irish Gaelic. At one time the word slob was used to describe muddy land, and that term came from the Gaelic *slab*, for mud, and the Swedish *slabb*, for slack. Muddy land would have been just as difficult for horses and wagons to navigate as the heavy masses of

S

floating ice, so the use of this term expanded onshore to refer to any sloppy, difficult conditions.

SNOOSE

Also known as chewing tobacco, snooze is a variety of moist snuff, the finely ground, smokeless tobacco that attained popularity during the 18th century. The origins of moist snuff can be traced to Scandinavia, notably Finland and Sweden, where it is still consumed in great amounts and is known as *snus*. Snoose, the anglicized version of that word, entered Canadian English in the late 19th century, when the first great wave of Scandinavian immigration to Canada occurred. Many came to work in the coalmines of British Columbia and to help build railways such as the Grand Trunk. Snoose was so prized and valued among these workers that in 1898, when Canadian railway builder Mike Heney was told that it was would be impossible to construct the White Pass and Yukon Railway to open up the gold fields of the Klondike, he simply said, "Give me Swedes and enough snoose, and I'll build a railway to hell." He did. He constructed one of the steepest narrow-gauge railways in the world, a line that climbs 873 m in just 32 km. In the 1920s, Finnish loggers at Red Lake, Ontario, refused to continue working when they learned that their supply of snoose had been depleted. "No snoose, no wood," is all they would say. Snoose is still a popular tobacco product in Canada today.

SNOWBLOWER

Arthur Simcard knew all too well the problems of navigating through large, snow-clogged routes. He grew up on a dairy farm and on days when snow-drifts were simply too large to surmount, he and his family would lose money as their milk sat, unsold and trapped, in the snow. Simcard began to look for a solution and remembered the wheat threshers he had seen, with their rotating blades that threw wheat into the machine itself. He began experimenting with various designs, and though he failed miserably a number of times, he persevered. In 1925, he unveiled his snowblowing device in Montréal, a four-wheel truck chassis with a snow scooper and a blower with two adjustable chutes that could toss snow 27 m. He called it the Simcard Snow Remover Snowblower, and in 1927 he sold a model to Outremont, a town near Montréal. Communities throughout Québec followed suit, as did Ottawa. Simcard, who had been previously dismissed as a hopeless dreamer, revolutionized the snow-removal industry, allowing cities to clear roads quickly and efficiently.

SPUD ISLAND

As Canada's largest supplier of potatoes, Prince Edward Island is known affectionately to many as Spud Island. With its rich sandy soil and long winters that refresh the earth, Prince Edward Island is uniquely suited to the growing of the tuber, producing 1.5 billion kg of potatoes a year, or one-third of all potatoes grown in Canada. Potatoes from Prince Edward Island are exported throughout North America and also to Venezuela, Italy, Ukraine, Portugal and Thailand. Of the $317 million dollars the island grossed in 2000, over $150 million was from potatoes. The most popular tuber on the island is the Russet Burbank, ideally suited for the production of French fries. The word spud has been in use since the 15th century, originally to describe a sharp, narrow blade used to cut through roots and dig up weeds. As a verb, a plant spuds when it produces new buds or branches. Its origins as slang for potato are not definitive, though many believe it originated in New Zealand English.

STANFIELD'S

Synonymous now with winter and long underwear, Stanfield's got its start in 1866 when Charles E. Stanfield sold his interests in the Tryon Woollen Mills in Tryon, Prince Edward Island, to his brother, so that four years later, he could open the Truro Woollen Mills in Truro, Nova Scotia. There, Stanfield produced woollen underwear of all sorts. He also developed and manufactured the first cardigan jackets and stockinettes in Canada, and he introduced heavy rib underwear to Canadians. In 1896 he sold the company to his two sons, who proceeded to streamline the operation by focusing solely upon knitted merchandise. Stanfield's sons developed the shrinkproof process for which Stanfield's would become famous. By then, the company, known formerly as Truro Knitting Mills Limited, became known as Stanfield's. In the 1950s, it introduced its signature thermal underwear, which made the family millions. Later, when they entered politics, the Stanfields became known as a sort of homebred version of the Kennedys in America. The underwear was, and is, immensely popular.

STANLEY CUP

In 1893, Frederick Arthur, Lord Stanley of Preston, Canada's governor general and son of the Earl of Derby, purchased a $50 silver punchbowl to be awarded to the top amateur Canadian hockey team. Lord Stanley had bought the trophy with the hopes of increasing hockey's popularity, which at the time was limited mostly to Ontario and Québec. The trophy was christened the Dominion Challenge Cup, though it would be remembered for its informal name, the Stanley Cup. It was first awarded to the Montréal Amateur Athletic Association in 1893, making it North America's oldest professional sporting trophy. It quickly became the symbol of hockey excellence and supremacy, and in what must surely have delighted Lord Stanley, hockey clubs sprang up all across the country. In 1910, the National Hockey Association, which was the forerunner to the National Hockey League, took possession of the cup, and in 1926, it was decided that the cup would be awarded only to National Hockey

S

League teams. The original cup was retired to the Hockey Hall of Fame in 1969, but its traditions continue. On the Stanley Cup are etched the names of every member of the winning team, and it is still given, for a day, to every member of that team. Lord Stanley never did see a championship hockey game—he returned to England in 1893.

STREET NURSE

In 1987, Vancouver began an outreach program designed to promote AIDS awareness and prevention among the drug users, prostitutes and homeless of its city streets. To do so, nurses were sent into the streets in mobile clinics to exchange needles and distribute condoms. Their jobs also entailed walking inner city neighbourhoods and interviewing street people to learn their sexual histories. If one happened to be HIV-positive, street nurses turned to the bars and motels in the area in an effort to find and convince former sex partners to get tested. Although labour-intensive, the work of the street nurses of Vancouver has become an indispensable part of the city's health care system.

STUBBLE JUMPER

Slang for a Canadian prairie farmer, stubble jumper is a term most commonly associated, negatively in some cases, with farmers from Saskatchewan. The term's origins are murky, but one assumes that it was borne out of the popular and unfortunate misconception that Saskatchewan is nothing but an agonizingly flat prairie, full of wheat, stubble and little else. Some Saskatchewanites consider it a term of pride.

STUBBY

Between 1961 and 1986, Canadian beer was bottled in a short, neckless bottle that became known as the stubby. It was eventually phased out in favour of the longneck bottles with twist-off caps that were so popular in the United States. Many Canadians still yearn for the stubby, and some breweries, recognizing this nostalgic longing, are re-introducing it.

STUPID LINE

Coined by the Canadian Injury Prevention Foundation (now known as SMARTRISK) on January 6, 1994, for a campaign aimed at helping people re-think risky behaviour, the stupid line is the metaphorical boundary distinguishing a smart risk from a stupid risk. The campaign used this tagline to spread its message: "We each have a line of choice that separates a smart risk from a stupid risk. The Stupid Line. Where will you draw yours?" It might be used, for example, when an individual in a drunken stupor phones a former girlfriend and proposes. He has crossed the stupid line.

S

SWISH

Its origins are unclear, but one can reasonably assume that for as long as whiskey and rum have been produced in Canada, so too has swish. When a rum or whiskey barrel had outlived its usefulness, distillers either tossed the barrels away or sold them to gardeners to use as planters. It wasn't long before some enterprising soul realized that by swishing boiling water in the barrel, alcohol could be extracted from the liquor-soaked wood. Some barrels could produce as many as 22 litres of hootch, with an alcohol content of anywhere from 12 percent to 40 percent. It certainly wasn't the best-tasting stuff around, but swish did the job of rum and whiskey on the cheap. The practice is still common today, and although it's not illegal, its sale is unlicensed and untaxed. In fact, the Alberta Gaming and Liquor Commission recently asked distillers to poison barrels sold to the public so that swish cannot be made.

TO GO OUTSIDE

For a long time, Canada's North lay relatively empty, with scattered communities of traders, hunters and First Nations eking out a hard-scrabble existence. Communication was slow and inefficient. Little has changed, and much of the English slang from the North reflects this sense of alienation and isolation. In the North, the outside refers to civilization; to go outside isn't just to step outside the front door, but to go from the Arctic to the more densely settled areas of the country. Not surprisingly, the North is referred to as "the inside."

TOBOGGAN

A toboggan refers to a long and narrow sled, made of thin boards curled upwards at one end. The word is derived from the Algonquin word, *odabaggan*, which originally described a sled made of bark used to drag game through the snow. One assumes that when they came to a hill, they hopped aboard the sled with their game. The Mi'kmaq called their version a *topaghan*, which early French Canadian

T

explorers translated into *tobagan*. The early Inuit made theirs out of whalebone.

TOGGY

Although not the most politically correct garment (it is made of beaverskin, after all), the toggy was popular at a time when keeping warm superceded all other concerns. Early Canada was built from the fur trade. Trappers and traders from the Hudson's Bay Company worked in the North, seeking the pelts and furs in demand throughout Europe. One of their favourite garments was the toggy, a calf-length coat made of either beaver or caribou skin. Its design was influenced by the Cree, who called their version the *misotaki*. Trappers and fur traders shortened it to toggy. The coats themselves were in much demand; after having been worn for a year, human body oils rendered the beaver skin rich and supple, the sort of skin popular with British hatmakers.

TOONIE

In February 1996, a new Canadian coin went into circulation. Like the loonie before it, the coin was designed to eliminate a paper bill. This time, the two-dollar bill was being taken out of circulation. Its replacement was a bimetallic coin, with an outer ring of mostly nickel and an inner ring of mostly copper. The inner ring depicts a polar bear crossing an ice floe in early summer; the image is meant to illustrate the diversity of geography and weather in

Canada. The process by which the bimetallic coin is joined together was patented by the Royal Canadian Mint, and while some of the earliest two-dollar coins were flawed (the inner copper ring could be easily dislodged), the errors have been corrected. Among the nicknames for the coin were the *bearly* and the *doubloonie*. One terrible punster came up with *The Queen with the Bear Behind*...quite a mouthful and sure to induce groaning. The name that stuck was toonie, a combination of two and loonie, the coin that preceded the toonie's introduction. This name did elicit groans of its own, but it has become a part of Canadian English.

TOONIK TYME

Since 1965, Iqaluit has celebrated the coming of spring and the return of the sun annually with its Toonik Tyme Festival. For a week, people gather to take part in a wide variety of events, old and new, including igloo-building, ice golf, drum dancing, throat singing, hockey and hunting events involving rabbits, seals and ptarmigans. Its name is derived from the Inuit word *tuniq*, given to the legendary giants of Cape Dorset in the southwest corner of Baffin Island who were said to have preceded the Inuit ancestors. An honorary tuniq roams Iqaluit each year during the festival dressed in an all-caribou outfit and mask. Those who spot him call the local CBC television station for a chance to win prizes.

TOURTIÈRE

Served at either Christmas Eve (usually at the Christmas feast, or reveillon, held the morning after midnight Mass) or on New Year's Eve, a tourtière is a traditional Québec meat pie dish. The tourtière, brought to New France by French explorers, draws its name from a medieval French pie dish used for cooking pigeons and other birds. The contents within were known as the *piece tourtière*; eventually, the name came to describe the meal as well. The tourtière can be made with a combination of beef, pork, lamb, veal or venison and a mixture of different spices, usually including cinnamon and cloves. Each region of Québec has its own special interpretations of this favourite dish.

TOUTIN

A popular breakfast item in Newfoundland, toutin is a sort of dough cake or flapjack. The dough is usually made the night before and then allowed to rest and rise. Cut into bite-sized pieces, the dough is fried in pork fat and then covered liberally with molasses and bits of pork. It was a favourite of woodsmen, who found that the toutin's high levels of fat prevented it from freezing as other foods might. There are almost as many variations on this dish as there are spellings for it: toutan, touten, touton, and towtent. One recipe calls for wrapping the dough pancake around a piece of bologna. Although some might find the dish a little fatty in these weight-conscious days, the meal still warms bellies on those frigid Atlantic coast days.

TRIVIAL PURSUIT

On December 15, 1979, *Montréal Gazette* photo editor Chris Haney and *Canadian Press* sportswriter Scott Abbott got together to play a game of Scrabble. Their set was missing pieces, so they decided to invent a game of their own. They eventually called the new game Trivial Pursuit, a board game that *Time* magazine called the "biggest phenomenon in game history." The first set of Trivial Pursuit, issued under the Horn Abbot Company, was sold in 1981. Although all 1100 copies sold out, toy buyers at the Montréal and New York toy fairs of 1982 seemed less than enthusiastic, placing orders for just 400 games. The company pressed on, finally garnering the attention of Chieftain Products, a Canadian subsidiary of a major American games company. In 1983, 2.3 million sets were sold in Canada, and a million sold in the United States. In 1984, Trivial Pursuit sales topped one billion dollars. Today, Trivial Pursuit continues to be one of the world's most popular board games. It is played in 19 languages in 33 different countries.

TULLIBEE

Early French Canadian fur traders named this small, delicately flavoured fish *toubibi*, a corruption of the Ojibwa *oto-lipi*. *Toubibi* was anglicized into tullibee, a relative of the whitefish that bears a striking resemblance to the sea herring. Used either as bait for lake trout or as food, tullibee is widely distributed throughout Canada, from the Mackenzie River to the Great Lakes and into Labrador. Also known as the cisco (*Coregonus artedii*) or the lake herring, the tullibee is often smoked for consumption.

TUQUE

As Canadian as maple syrup and Canada Day, this knitted, sock-like cap is said to have been the invention of cold European sailors, who created it to keep their heads warm on long ocean voyages. A little controversy surrounds the origins of this word. Some believe that *tuque* is a variant of the Québec French word *toque*, which is supposedly derived from the French verb *toquer*, meaning "to knock" (the original tuque had a long, drooping end that tended to knock its wearer on the back of the neck.) Other sources suggest the word is based on the word *tukka*, a pre-Latin word meaning "gourd or hill," presumably because of the tuque's conical shape. Still others claim the word is a shortened, anglicized version of the Chinook Jargon word *latuk*, which means "woollen cap." However you wear it, the tuque is a practical, if not always aesthetically pleasing, winter garment that no Canadian closet should be without.

VICO

Like Ovaltine and Horlick's, Vico made its name producing and selling a chocolate malted drink. Although few have probably heard of the stuff, it has found a huge number of fans in Saskatchewan, where Vico is a generic term that refers to all chocolate milk.

WHISKEY-JACK

Also called the moose bird, the camp robber or the
Canada jay, the whiskey-jack (*Perisoreus canadensis*)
is a grey bird common throughout the coniferous
forests of Canada. It is known as a voracious eater,
fond of almost everything edible and some things
not so edible. It is often spotted near campgrounds,
where its habit of stealing food has earned it its
not-so-flattering nickname. Its name is derived
from a mispronunciation of the Cree name for the
bird, *weskuchanis,* meaning "little blacksmith." Early
English trappers heard whiskey-jack and the name
stuck. The bird tends to use its saliva to glue meat,
suet and whatever else it can find from a campsite
into balls, which it then hides among pine needles
near its nest.

WHOOP-UP

The whoop-up has its origins in southern Alberta
where, near Lethbridge, there once stood a notorious fort. Since 1832, it had been illegal to sell
alcohol to aboriginals in the United States. Unde-
terred, whiskey traders from Montana headed

north to Canada. In 1869, using Fort Benton as a supply post, two men, John Healy and Alfred Hamilton, built Fort Hamilton in southern Alberta. From there, they traded whiskey to the Natives. The liquor proved especially popular after the great herds of buffalo had been decimated. Ingredients such as soap, red ink and tobacco went into the brews, which acquired names such as "fire water," "red eye," "bug juice" and "whoop-up wallop." The fort burned to the ground in 1870, but was rebuilt that same year and rechristened Fort Whoop-Up to continue its business. Fort Whoop-Up was a plague upon the land until Canadian Prime Minister John A. Macdonald sent the North-West Mounted Police to bring order to the prairies. After 1875, Fort Whoop-Up was used only as an outpost, but its reputation survived.

WINNIPEG GOLDEYE

A freshwater fish, the Winnipeg goldeye (*Hiodon alosoides*) was named for its gold-coloured eyes and because Lake Winnipeg was the largest producer of the fish. Long a part of the diet of the Cree and other First Nations tribes, European explorers found the goldeye flesh soft and tasteless. But sometime in the late 19th century, someone noticed that Natives often smoked and cured the fish before consuming it, and an industry was born. For a time, smoked Winnipeg goldeye became a popular luxury item, with demand far exceeding supply. But by the 1920s, stocks of the fish in Lake Winnipeg dwindled to almost nothing as a result of overfishing. Today, Winnipeg goldeye is fished mainly in the North and South Saskatchewan rivers, although the fish is still processed and smoked over oak fires almost exclusively in Winnipeg. The Winnipeg goldeye is a small fish, just 30.5 cm long, with a dark-blue to blue-green back, silver sides and a white belly. Like those of a cat, the goldeye's eyes reflect light.

WOBBLY WOBBLY

Established in 1905, Industrial Workers of the World, or the IWW, is also known as the Wobbly Wobbly. Although the union was created in Chicago, its nickname has distinctly Canadian roots. In 1912, railway workers and members of the IWW went on strike. Up until that time, they had been called everything from International Wonder Workers to I Won't Works. As the IWW was one of the first unions that didn't deny membership to Chinese Canadians or Chinese Americans, the IWW had much support among Vancouver's Chinese population. Among them was a restaurateur who, legend has it, offered free food and credit to members of the striking IWW. He asked strikers coming into his restaurant, in thickly accented English, if they were in the "I Wobbly Wobbly." The name struck a chord with the strikers, who adopted it as their own. Mortimer Downing, an IWW member, stated in a 1923 letter, perhaps with a little overstatement, that the nickname "hints of a fine, practical international-ism, a human brotherhood based on a community of interests and of understanding." Not bad for a simple mispronunciation.

WONDERBRA

The Wonderbra, like the Canadarm, revolutionized the world—a Wonderbra is sold every 15 seconds. Canadian designer Louise Poirier invented it in 1964; the etymology of the word should be obvious. It had 54 design elements, all working to validate the bra's full name: The Wonderbra Push-up Plunge Bra. Poirier fashioned the device for the Canadian lingerie company Canadelle, which became a part of the Playtex family, itself a subsidiary of Sara Lee. Sara Lee introduced the Wonderbra to the United States in 1994 to great acclaim and popularity; it appeared on year-end Top 10 Product lists in *Newsweek, Fortune, Time* and *USA Today*. Who says Canadians are known just for maple syrup and hockey? We can add The Wonderbra Push-Up Plunge Bra to the list.

XY COMPANY

With the signing of the Treaty of Paris in 1763, the French fur traders of Montréal found their practice and business choked off by the newly emboldened Hudson's Bay Company and the burgeoning ranks of Scottish businessmen in the city. Their livelihood threatened, Montréal fur traders realized that solidarity was critical and made several aborted attempts to form a company of their own. Finally, in the winter of 1783, a group of traders, led by Simon McTavish, created the North West Company, beginning a period of intense rivalry and bitter competition that lasted almost forty years. But while its main competitor was the Hudson's Bay Company, the North West Company faced foment from within. In 1795, a reorganization of the company created dissension and resentment between North West Company agents and its winterers— the men who braved harsh conditions to trade with the Native population. In 1798, embittered and disillusioned, the alienated winterers created the New North West Company. To distinguish their goods from those of the North West Company, the

New North West Company marked its bales with an XY. The business became known as the XY Company. Although the XY Company did reach as far as the Athabasca in 1798, the competition was devastating for both. Liquor use among agents and winterers skyrocketed, as did wages. In 1804, McTavish, the man many held responsible for the necessity of the XY Company, died and tensions between the two gradually dissolved. In November, the two companies merged, and the XY Company receded into history. The North West Company shared a similar fate in 1821 when the British government, embarrassed and at the end of its patience following the fighting at the Red River Colony, forced the squabbling North West Company and Hudson's Bay Company to merge.

YUKON GOLD

The Yukon Gold potato was the first Canadian potato to be marketed and bred by name, and it is truly a potato of the people. Before the introduction of the Yukon Gold, Canada's potatoes usually had a white flesh that was unfamiliar to new arrivals, who much preferred the yellow-fleshed tubers of their homelands. The only problem was that no one had managed to create an enhanced, disease-resistant, gold variety potato that could prosper in the North American climate. At least, not until Dr. Gary Johnston set about finding a solution. Beginning in the late 1960s, Johnston, with funding from Agriculture and Agri-Food Canada, began work on developing a gold potato at the University of Guelph. For 13 years Johnston toiled. Finally, in 1980, he succeeded with a crossbreed of a North American white potato and a wild South American yellow potato. He called it the Yukon Gold, and it soon became the favourite potato of chefs and gourmets. Although the white potato of North America still remains the most popular tuber sold, the Yukon Gold is quickly gaining popularity.

ZIPPER

Some may argue that Swedish-born Canadian immigrant Gideon Sundback is not the true father of the zipper. After all, Elias Howe and Whitcomb Judson, both Americans, had patented fastening devices to replace the inefficient buttons that were used to close pants and jackets. But the inventions of Howe and Judson proved wildly unpopular. Howe chose not to market his device, and when Judson unveiled his "Clasp Locker" to the public at the 1893 Chicago World's Fair, he sold only 20 to the United States Postal Service. It took a marriage and Gideon Sundback to usher the zipper into the modern age. At Judson's Universal Fastener Company, Sundback's design skills came to the attention of the factory foreman, who was Sundback's father-in-law. Sundback became Universal's head designer, responsible for improving the design of its Clasp Locker. After his wife's untimely death in 1911, Sundback channelled his grief into his work, and in 1913, unveiled his "Separate Fastener." He had increased the number of fasteners from four per inch to 10 or 11 and widened the opening for

Z

the glider's teeth. Although his design wasn't perfect (the fastener tended to rust), Sundback had created something unique and was issued a patent for his design in 1917. The initial reaction to the zipper was tepid, and almost 20 years passed before the zipper would become commonplace. In 1923, B.F. Goodrich ordered 150,000 of Sundback's devices for use in his new product: the rubber galosh. Goodrich loved the hookless fasteners, and even more, loved the sound they made. He began calling them zippers, and the name stuck. In the 1930s, zippers in children's clothing were promoted as a means of helping children become more independent; the fashion industry took notice and began using the device. By the late 1930s, French clothing designers were raving about Sundback's invention. *Esquire* magazine called it the "Newest Tailoring Idea for Men." Today, Sundback's "Separate Fastener" is found everywhere with thousands of zipper miles produced each day.

Z